Start Your Own

CATERING

Business

Start Your Own

CATERING

Business

PRENTICE HALL
Paramus, New Jersey 07652

Printed in the United States of America

10 9 8 7 6 5 4 3

This publication is designed to provide accurate and authoritative information in regard to the subject matter covered. It is sold with the understanding that the publisher is not engaged in rendering legal, accounting, or other professional service. If legal advice or other expert assistance is required, the services of a competent professional person should be sought.
—*From the Declaration of Principles jointly adopted by a Committee of the American Bar Association and a Committee of Publishers and Associations*

ISBN 0-13-603309-1

ATTENTION: CORPORATIONS AND SCHOOLS

Prentice Hall books are available at quantity discounts with bulk purchase for educational, business, or sales promotional use. For information, please write to: Prentice Hall Career & Personal Development Special Sales, 240 Frisch Court, Paramus, New Jersey 07652. Please supply: title of book, ISBN number, quantity, how the book will be used, date needed.

PRENTICE HALL
Career & Personal Development
Paramus, NJ 07652
A Simon & Schuster Company

On the World Wide Web at http://www.phdirect.com

Prentice-Hall International (UK) Limited, *London*
Prentice-Hall of Australia Pty. Limited, *Sydney*
Prentice-Hall Canada Inc., *Toronto*
Prentice-Hall Hispanoamericana, S.A., *Mexico*
Prentice-Hall of India Private Limited, *New Delhi*
Prentice-Hall of Japan, Inc., *Tokyo*
Simon & Schuster Asia Pte. Ltd., *Singapore*
Editora Prentice-Hall do Brasil, Ltda., *Rio de Janeiro*

CONTENTS

PREFACE

Start Your Own Catering Business is the result of many hours of in-depth research into the mail order industry. Our exclusive team of National Business Library's professional business writers has brought years of practical experience to this project, and we know that the information provided in this book will set you on the road to success.

Owning your own business can be the most exciting and rewarding venture you will ever experience. We talk of hundreds of small business owners who make comments like, "Doing something I really enjoy makes every new day a pleasure," or "If I had known I could be realizing this kind of income, rather than making my former boss wealthy, I would have started my own business years ago."

It's true! You'll never get rich working for someone else. By capitalizing on your experience, investing time and energy, and studying the proven techniques and business methods provided in this book, you will be well on the way to realizing your goals for success in your own venture. It takes courage to begin. Without a doubt, the first step is the hardest—and you have already taken it.

INTRODUCTION:
COOKING UP PROFITS

If you have a flair for working with food and enjoy the thought of entertaining several nights a week, there is incredible profit potential for you in the booming catering business.

The number of people who opt to have their gatherings catered by a professional service has never been greater. This trend is due both to the resurgence of business and social entertaining and to the increased number of women in the work force. Women have been the primary coordinators and cooks of such functions in the past, but career demands have made hiring someone to handle these tasks a necessity.

And, of course, there are the traditional wedding receptions, bridal and baby showers, anniversary celebrations and coming-of-age events that go more smoothly for the host if the food planning and preparation is taken care of by a caterer.

With the cost per person or per serving ranging from $15 to $50 depending on the menu and other variables covered in this book, and food costs averaging 25 percent to 30 percent, the profit potential in catering can run as high as 50 percent—especially if you plan to start the business in your home kitchen and do most

of the work yourself. Some catering services that specialize in gourmet cuisine handle only a few events per month and realize gross profits of 70 percent and annual incomes of up to $250,000!

There are a number of ways to set up your catering enterprise based on a business plan that is comfortable and feasible. You can keep it simple by setting up at home and focusing primarily on the preparation of food, while leaving the serving responsibilities to the host. You can also only accept jobs that allow you to handle the majority of the preparation and cooking tasks at the site of the event. Alternatively, you can open the business in a commercial location and hire a staff of cooks and servers to work on an "as-needed" basis.

The information provided in this book will help you work your way through the start-up process. It will help you structure your catering business, offer additional services to your clientele, establish a fee schedule, and create menus for a wide range of occasions.

People are not about to stop entertaining, but they are likely to stop trying to coordinate all the steps involved once they know about your new service. Build a successful business doing something that you love, and enjoy the raves of satisfied clients and their guests!

1

THE GROWTH OF
SMALL BUSINESS

The 1980s were referred to as America's "entrepreneurial era." In 1986, more than 750,000 new businesses were created in the United States. In 1989, more than a million new ventures were started nationwide—almost half of them by women. In 1991, there were 20.5 million small businesses in the United States—and the entrepreneurial era is continuing through the 1990s. The recession of the early 1990s compelled suddenly unemployed people to start their own businesses in order to survive. An upsurge in part-time businesses has also fueled an entrepreneurial trend, with people in search of extra income working on profitable ventures during their off-hours.

More and more people are opting to leave their 9-to-5 jobs and stop "making someone else rich" to focus their energies on building a successful business of their own. The combined circumstances of fewer advancement opportunities, lack of job security, and the possibility of retiring without a pension are also driving the trend toward self-employment.

Today, the number of individuals who are self-employed is at its highest level ever, and based on your interest in this book, it's

quite possible that you'll be joining the ranks of small business owners in the near future. It may be simply a dream right now, but that's how these businesses start.

> *You can never be too young, too old, too busy, or too poor to start a business.*

Starting and operating your own small business is one of the most exciting and satisfying challenges you can undertake. There are no limitations on income potential when you're investing time and energy in your own enterprise. With the practical information provided in this book and dedication to your business goals, your chances for success are excellent.

What Is a Small Business?

The majority of businesses in the United States today are classified as small businesses. The definitions of what constitutes a small business run the gamut from the size of the overall staff (typically under 100) to the amount of assets or sales volume. However, in this book, small business is defined as one that is independently owned and operated.

The major benefit of this type of business is that you have the ability to make decisions quickly and act on them immediately. What typically bogs down big business is the number of people involved in the decision-making process.

Other advantages include the fact that small businesses can provide personalized service to the community or the market they're serving and the owner has the freedom, independence, and control to operate exactly as he or she chooses.

It's important to remember, however, that most major corporations, from Ford Motor Company and McDonald's to Mary Kay Cosmetics, started out as small businesses—as dreams.

It was because of basic business sense and a willingness to learn and adapt as their companies grew that Henry Ford, Ray Kroc, and Mary Kay, and thousands like them, steered their dreams into monumental financial successes.

Whether your goal is to supplement an existing income and to operate a solely owned home-based business from your garage, kitchen table, or spare bedroom, or to start a business that involves raising substantial capital, finding and setting up a commercial location, and hiring employees, you have the potential to enjoy an independent lifestyle that carries with it a number of rewards. And the rewards are as varied as the people who pursue them.

Accepting the Challenge

Remember, these rewards do not come without hard work and the willingness to research and understand all facets of running your business. Many new businesses fail within the first few years.

Reasons given for the early demise of a small business range from lack of organization or management experience to undercapitalization, misunderstanding of the importance of advertising, inexperience in pricing products and services, lack of an overall business plan, improper hiring practices, and failure to accurately assess the competition.

Entrepreneur
A person who undertakes an independent enterprise; one who has made the decision to go into business for him/herself.

It isn't that someone purposely starts a business without having explored these areas. However, many times a person feels that his or her demonstrated expertise while in the employ of another can easily be transferred into a personal business. This is only partially true.

While it is imperative that you have particular skills or talents—because selling them is what your ultimate success will be based on—it's equally important to understand how to sell them, to know exactly what your profit margin is, and what steps you need to take to ensure the continued growth of your business.

Sounds easy, right? It really can be. But like anything else worth doing, starting your own business means careful planning. For example, you wouldn't consider taking a month-long vacation without doing some serious planning to ensure that the house was

taken care of while you were gone, that you had made reservations for lodging, tours, and flights, and that you had converted your cash into traveler's checks.

There are so many aspects involved in running a business, it is vital to be prepared for any eventuality. Being prepared means being informed, so that when situations do arise you know how to deal with them.

Is "Failure" Really Failure?

We have all heard stories about people who started their businesses on a shoestring and who became successful because of their sheer determination to make it work. It does happen, but these people are the exception rather than the rule, and in most cases have had experts standing behind them to give them guidance when problems came up. Others fail and, unfortunately, this often holds potential new business owners back. We hear and read about amazingly high figures related to so-called business failures.

According to a research project conducted by Albert Shapero, professor of the American Free Enterprise System at Ohio State University for many years, no one really knows the true failure rate of new businesses. The main reason for this is because there is not really a standard definition of "failure" in this case. He points out that a number of businesses close for a variety of reasons, many of which are not documented.

For example, in some cases the owners reach retirement age and have no one to pass the business along to; others shut down because the owners simply get bored; while still other entrepreneurs file a Chapter 11 bankruptcy, which basically gives them the opportunity to stay in business and continue operating under a court-approved plan, even though they become a statistic on the "failure" list.

The other extremely important aspect to consider when thinking about the benefits and risks of starting your own business is that having a business fail has never been a deterrent for true entrepreneurs. Many well-known business moguls failed at least once, and often more than once, before striking it rich.

Learning From Experience

In fact, almost anyone who has had a business fail will tell you that the experience was more valuable than anything they could have been taught in a business school and provided them with the knowledge they needed to start another venture successfully. This kind of determination is a valid qualification for self-employment and will pay off handsomely.

When you own your own business, you are responsible for everything. There will be times, such as when your accounts receivable are running sixty days late or the phone company puts the wrong number in your Yellow Pages listing, that returning to the 9-to-5 world will seem like a tempting option.

This is where self-discipline, an unwavering belief in your product or service, and the determination to be your own boss will pull you through.

But, again, we can't stress enough the importance of planning, understanding basic business practices, being aware of consumer trends, and taking the time to develop, implement, and update goals to ensure success for your efforts.

What This Book Offers

This book is designed to provide you with the information you will need to start your catering business, to offer techniques to help you with day-to-day operations, and to provide anecdotes about people just like you who had a dream and, through planning and determination, were able to turn that dream into a successful reality.

In addition to focusing on aspects of the catering business, we cover such important business matters as

♦ Recognizing the entrepreneurial profile

♦ Taking our exclusive Entrepreneurial Quiz

♦ Finding the right audience for your business through easy marketing techniques

♦ Organizing for efficiency

♦ Recognizing legalities

- ◆ Addressing financial concerns
- ◆ Getting your home office up and running
- ◆ Charting your enterprise's growth

You will find specific how-to information on

- ◆ Advertising and promoting your business
- ◆ Finding capital
- ◆ Saving money on operating expenses
- ◆ Developing a simple bookkeeping system that will show you whether you're facing a financial crisis or realizing a profit

You're never too young, too old, too busy, or too poor to start a business. Owning your own business means taking advantage of our marvelous system of free enterprise. Earning a substantial living and, even better, realizing a profit for doing something you enjoy is the American dream come true.

The road to financial independence through self-employment is challenging and rewarding.

The opportunities for entrepreneurs have never been better. Armed with a solid product or service to sell, the determination to succeed and, most important, business know-how, there is nothing that can stand in your way.

Notes

Key Points

Personal Thoughts

Additional Research

2

THE ENTREPRENEURIAL PROFILE

Starting a business is one thing, making it work is another. We know that success in self-employment is largely the result of careful planning and an understanding of basic business techniques and formulas.

As many successful entrepreneurs claim, making money doing something you love is the best way to ensure a profitable future. It is always easier to address the inevitable business challenges that crop up when you are creating a product or providing a service that gives you a sense of pleasure and personal satisfaction.

Start a business based on your expertise in a specific field and focus your involvement in an area that you thoroughly enjoy.

Personality is a significant factor in determining what kind of business to get involved in, the way you will eventually set up the legal structure (sole proprietorship, partnership, etc.), and how you will run the business on a day-to-day basis. For example, if you are planning to start a business that is based on your artistic or creative abilities, it is possible that your personality is not suited

to the very important aspect of sales. But without strong selling abilities, there is a likelihood that your goal of distributing, for example, your hand-carved wooden boxes nationally will not come to fruition.

This isn't to say that you should decide against going into business for yourself. It simply indicates that it would be in your best interest to join forces with someone who does have strong selling skills, who believes in the product as much as you do, and who will work with you toward a common goal.

On the other hand, if your personality is geared to working with people, it is a good idea to consider a business that will emphasize this ability, such as developing seminars or workshops based on your area of expertise, providing independent counseling or tutoring, or providing a service such as gift-basket designing or catering, which depends on your interaction with people on a one-to-one or a group basis for success.

Research shows that in order to address the many and varied situations that arise in business ownership, the true entrepreneur should possess the following personality traits.

Ten Important Entrepreneurial Traits

1. Self-awareness	6. Decisiveness
2. Self-motivation	7. Experience
3. Courage	8. Knowledge
4. Confidence	9. Perseverance
5. Patience	10. Drive

1. ***Self-awareness.*** Know who you are, what you're good at, and what you like to do. Start a business that is based on your expertise in a specific field and focus your involvement in an area that you thoroughly enjoy.

2. ***Self-motivation.*** Self-motivation is one of the most important personality traits of successful entrepreneurs. This is the characteristic that gets you going and keeps you moving when you are in business for yourself. It's what helps you to keep turning out those craft items, upgrading your technical skills, or developing new and improved promotional techniques when business is slow. It's what gives you the tenacity and confidence to call on a potential client even though you've heard "No" three times.

 Self-motivation is also what helps you overcome the fears and concerns that inevitably arise when you own your own business. It is the main ingredient that has spurred on people who have achieved success despite drawbacks, such as minimal capital, lack of education, or limited experience.

 People with a high degree of self-motivation see the greatest obstacles, such as learning a new aspect of business management, as a new and exciting challenge to overcome. If you've ever undertaken a project without fully understanding the mechanics involved in performing the task or knowing what the outcome would be, you were operating on self-motivation—the conviction that you would be able to learn whatever was needed to accomplish your goal.

 And regardless of the outcome of the project, you undoubtedly gained more experience and knowledge than you had before, which only works to increase your sense of motivation to handle new challenges.

3. ***Courage.*** Courage or the willingness to take risks is a valuable trait when striving for success. A successful person might say something like: "I don't know how I did it; I just made a phone call and asked for the money I needed." It was more than luck that made it possible for this person to raise the needed capital to get a business off the ground; it was the willingness to take a chance and hope for a positive response to the request.

The owner of a small cabinet-refinishing business said, "I always figure that the worst thing that can happen is someone will say no, so it never hurts to try." In the game of business, you must be willing to take chances. Even if you don't get exactly what you want every time, the odds are good that if you feel strongly about what you need, you will get it. But you have to ask!

4. **Confidence.** The age-old philosophy of positive thinking is a major step in the direction of success. By behaving as if you already are a success at what you do, it follows that you will be, and your customers will believe it, too. A confident attitude is one of the most appealing traits you can exhibit to prospective clients, for it lets them know that they will be getting the best their money can buy.

5. **Patience.** When you own your own business, there will be times when you feel like the roof is caving in, especially when your suppliers seem to be taking their own sweet time in fulfilling an important order or when a customer's demands seem to be unrealistic. Although you may be able to hurry the supplier along, you must remember that your customers are always right, since they are the ones who will make or break your business.

> *You have to accept whatever comes, and the important thing is that you meet it with courage and with the best you have to give.*
>
> *Eleanor Roosevelt*

If you are aware that patience is not your strong suit, develop a stop-gap exercise to use at times when coping is a definite necessity. Whether you count to ten before saying a word, visualize a pleasant scene, or repeat a secret phrase to yourself when tension is running high, it will be to your advantage.

6. **Decisiveness.** Business has been described as a process of making one fast decision after another. Often, a decision has to be made immediately, on the spur of the

moment. In those instances, you should go with your intuition and trust that you are doing the right thing.

However, if you are the type of person who prefers to analyze your options, weigh all the factors, and make decisions slowly, then that is what you must do. It will keep your confidence intact and ensure that you're taking the right action. Again, careful planning will help you predict many of the decision-making situations that arise in your business. As time goes by and you grow more comfortable in your role as a business owner, you will undoubtedly find yourself making quicker decisions.

7. ***Experience.*** A primary reason some businesses fail within a few years of start-up is lack of business experience. Whether or not your experience is directly related to the business you are planning to start, it is a key component for growth.

If you feel you do not have enough business experience, there are several avenues you can take before starting your own enterprise. Returning to school for specialized courses is one consideration. Most community colleges and adult education facilities offer classes and seminars in business start-up and maintenance, and there are hundreds of home-study or correspondence courses that will, in many cases, give you official certification in your field.

However, your best solution is to take a job in the field you're interested in. By asking questions about all the aspects of the business, you will gain experience, get paid for learning, and find out whether this is really what you want to do before sinking money, time, and energy into the enterprise.

8. ***Knowledge.*** Experience in your field is invaluable, but it is not enough. You have a better chance of succeeding the more you know about such vital factors as business basics, the product or service that you want to sell, the industry you are entering, your competition, and the local, regional, state, and/or national markets. Do your homework.

9. ***Perseverance.*** One of the adages you will hear time and time again when talking to entrepreneurs is that perseverance is 90 percent of the battle to succeed.

 If you are like the majority of new small business owners, the entire staff and support system for your venture is probably *you*. Making a dream come true can be a lonely task, especially when you are just getting started, and ensuring that it works often means little rest or relaxation. You must be willing to persevere during the rough times, to hang in there during the slow periods, and to maintain your belief in your product or service—even when it seems like no one else in the world knows you exist. It has been written that through perseverance the snail reached the ark. So it is with success!

10. ***Drive.*** You must believe in your goal and be determined to succeed. The successful businessperson does not view obstacles or stumbling blocks as problems, but rather as challenges. To make your business a success, you need to be totally committed and willing to work long hours, especially in the beginning. If you do not have the time or commitment to dedicate to your dream, then you are better off working for someone else.

The Entrepreneurial A to Z Appraisal

Owning a business calls for the ability to handle different situations with confidence. The following self-appraisal quiz has no right or wrong answers. It is designed to help you determine certain personality traits, attitudes, and qualifications that will benefit you in your venture. Upon completion, use the appraisal as a starting point for discussions with friends and family members about your business profile. Acknowledging your strong and weak points will help you prepare for your role as an entrepreneur.

Entrepreneurial Quiz

Use the letter *S* for strong or *N* for needs improvement beside the characteristics listed below. Give yourself sufficient time to analyze each trait.

Achievement: I have a strong desire to be successful in my chosen business venture. _____

Belief: I have faith in myself and the service or product I am specializing in to build my business. _____

Creativity: I am able to address situations in imaginative and innovative ways to reach my goals. _____

Discipline: I am self-motivated and can handle necessary tasks, whether or not I enjoy them. _____

Efficient: I am organized and can arrange my priorities or change my work methods as needed for maximum production. _____

Friendly: I am genuinely interested in people and enjoy my interactions with them on a day-to-day basis. _____

Goal Oriented: I have a tendency to set my sights on preset goals and will work hard toward achieving them. _____

Health Conscious: I am aware of my physical abilities and have the insight to work smart in order to preserve my health. _____

Independent: I am able to work alone, if necessary, and am willing to be responsible for my own actions. _____

Judgment: My conclusions about people or situations are generally accurate. _____

Knowledge: I have solid experience in my field and have spent enough time in a professional business setting to know the ropes. _____

Leadership: I am able to direct people effectively while instilling confidence and loyalty. _____

Maturity: I am willing to work toward long-term goals and do not get upset by the inevitable minor setbacks. _____

Networking: I am willing to develop associations with other entrepreneurs for professional support in my venture. _____

Optimism: I am able to see what is right about a situation and to explore its potential to the fullest. _____

Positive Attitude: I am convinced that I can accomplish anything I set my mind to, and rarely entertain negative thoughts. _____

Questioning: I am not afraid to ask questions to get the information I need to expand my knowledge. _____

Resourceful: I am able to find ways to accomplish just about any task I must do. _____

Sales Ability: I am able to present information about myself and/or my business in a convincing yet honest manner. _____

Tolerance: I am able to handle stressful situations with a positive and realistic attitude. _____

Undaunted Spirit: I am unafraid of the unknown. In fact, I enjoy a challenge and accept the consequences of my actions. _____

Venturesome: I am not afraid of hard work to reach my goals and enjoy finding new, positive ways to handle troublesome situations. _____

Well Balanced: I generally maintain a sense of humor when things don't work out as expected. _____

Expressive: I am able to express ideas and feelings clearly and logically, both orally and in written form. _____

Youthful Nature: I am capable of tackling work with enthusiasm and a high level of energy.

Zest: I look forward to enjoying my business, the people I will be dealing with, and the resulting fruits of my labor.

Scoring

Although this is merely a tool to provide you with information about your entrepreneurial profile, there are immediate clues to your future as a business owner in the responses you have given.

Add up your number of *S* responses and read the following interpretation that corresponds to the number you scored.

♦ **15+:** There is a good possibility that you have been involved in your own business in the past or, at least, have worked in a managerial capacity for someone else. You have the positive personality traits required to be a successful business owner.

♦ **8–14:** You are basically a positive and directed person and should not have any problem with improving certain areas to increase your personal business success potential.

♦ **0–7:** This is an indication that finding a complementary business partner who can support your goals may be an option worth considering.

Notes

Key Points

Personal Thoughts

Additional Research

3

STARTING YOUR
CATERING BUSINESS

Americans love to eat and entertain. But many of them have neither the time nor the talent to put together a function that is guaranteed to get raves. This is where the professional caterer steps in.

Caterers across the nation are cooking up incredible profits taking care of such details as planning a menu, preparing the food, setting up tables and serving guests for clients who willingly pay an average of $15 per person for the service. It is possible to realize gross profits of 20 percent to 50 percent on standard, easy-to-prepare dishes and even more–from 30 percent to 70 percent–on gourmet cuisine.

Overview of the Catering Business

Catering is a labor-intensive business with strong income potential and steady growth. It does not lend itself to absentee ownership and can be started from home with the owner as sole employee.

Minimum Start-up Investment:	**$100**
Average Start-up Investment:	**$5,000**
High Start-up Investment:	**$75,000**
Break-even Point:	**Immediate to six months**
Average Annual Gross Revenues:	**$50,000-$150,000**
Potential Annual Gross Revenues:	**$500,000**

It has become accepted practice for business people to entertain prospective and established clients as a means of showing appreciation and solidifying new contacts. Charitable and political organizations typically host catered open houses when campaigning for operating capital and support. And no traditional wedding or bar mitzvah would be a memorable event without the food and service provided by a conscientious caterer.

A number of restaurants have climbed on the catering bandwagon. The owner of Farmer Boy, a restaurant that serves meals from 6 a.m. to 3 p.m., takes advantage of the large kitchen facility and uses it as the base for his catering company.

All food is prepared after normal restaurant hours and delivered to clients at the location of their choice. Off-duty waitresses from the restaurant earn extra income by working the events as serving staff. The owner claims the catering business is more profitable than the restaurant!

Many small catering companies that support two owner/operators, often a husband and wife team, net $2,500 per week per owner. One couple works only weekends in a high-income area and claims to be clearing $5,000 net income per month!

Not Just a Flash in the Pan

The National Restaurant Association, in its *1995 Food Service Industry Forecast,* reports that revenues from social catering services (businesses whose sole operation is catering, i.e., no restaurants that also cater) were just over $2.5 billion in 1992 and projects that revenues for 1995 will be in excess of $3 billion. It comes as no surprise, then, that some solely-owned and operated, part-time catering businesses in various parts of the country pull in gross profits of up to 60 percent.

By using your home kitchen to prepare food, shopping carefully, renting or borrowing equipment during the early start-up days, and doing most of the work yourself, you can expect the same financial figures. Even caterers who invest in fully-equipped kitchens in commercial locations and hire staff on a regular basis realize a gross profit of up to 45 percent.

While some caterers choose to offer their services only for those occasions that they personally enjoy (such as weddings, parties or gourmet dinners for small groups), the most profitable caterers are willing to provide their services for a greater variety of situations. For most, flexibility is key to staying busy and in high demand.

> *Gardens were not made by singing "Oh, how beautiful" and sitting in the shade.*
> Rudyard Kipling

Many highly successful catering firms started as a partnership—an arrangement that seems to work extremely well in this business when the compatibility of partners is strong. Typically, one partner handles the cooking and serving operations while the other recruits business, handles the accounting and management tasks, and provides backup support wherever needed during the catered functions.

With little more than an interest in food, a willingness to work hard and the business basics outlined in this guide, you can make a profit with your very first catering job. Within one year, you can have an established reputation and be on your way to owning a larger operation if you choose.

Advantages of the Business

The majority of caterers interviewed for this book were motivated by the following factors:

◆ **Low Start-Up.** Throughout the country, there are successful catering services that were started with very little capital. Because catering is a service provided in a prearranged location, and because supplies can generally be found in your own kitchen, it is possible to get your first job for under $100.

A perfect example of this type of start-up is illustrated by the experience of Jill W. of Los Angeles, California. She catered her first dinner party at the request of a friend who knew she loved to cook. Jill used the friend's kitchen and equipment, and purchased the food with a "deposit" offered by her friend. In this auspicious first night, Jill made a net profit of $250. One year, her company grossed $800,000, boasted a full-time staff of ten, and catered between twenty-five and thirty-five events per week!

◆ **High Profit Potential.** Despite its low-risk appeal, catering offers the potential for high earnings if the service is promoted well and the business is carefully budgeted. Caterers charge anywhere from $10 to $50 per person, depending on the menu, the region of the country, and the services provided. Through careful planning, you can build profits quickly, starting with your first catering job.

◆ **Creativity.** If you enjoy cooking, you know that half the fun is in creating new recipes. Your ability to develop unique dishes and attractively serve them will put you in high demand. Discriminating hosts and entertainers are constantly on the lookout for something new and exciting to share with friends and business associates.

◆ **Flexible Hours.** Catering is a great fit for someone interested in starting a part-time business. The majority of catered affairs are held at night or on weekends, making it

feasible for the caterer to work another job while getting established. Though working nights and weekends can conflict with family responsibilities, many caterers have found creative solutions—planning family activities during non-working hours or involving family members in the business whenever possible.

♦ **Meeting People.** Caterers frequently mention how much they enjoy the interesting people they meet on the job. Through their work, caterers come into contact with people from a variety of backgrounds, many of whom they might not otherwise meet. And because this business thrives on word-of-mouth recommendations, the more contacts made by the caterer, the greater the potential for growth and success.

♦ **Personal Satisfaction.** Caterers have a unique opportunity to be present at celebrations of meaningful milestones—weddings, retirements, birthdays—in the lives of their clients. By making these events all the more special and carefree for the hosts, caterers are rewarded intrinsically as well as financially.

The Disadvantages

The drawbacks of the catering business are minimal in comparison with other service-oriented ventures, especially if the caterer uses a home kitchen or other existing kitchen space. Perhaps the biggest stress for caterers is the high-pressure, last-minute detail work. It isn't unusual for caterers and their assistants to work furiously preparing appetizers and desserts, while chopping, slicing, and parboiling ingredients for main courses, and mentally preparing for the last-minute cooking. Careful planning, however, can reduce this stress and ensure that everything that must be done is done in the proper sequence.

Other drawbacks of the catering business are the late hours, working weekends (most parties, weddings, and other social events take place on Saturdays and Sundays), and back strain from lifting and transporting heavy platters and supplies.

What Is Expected of a Caterer

Once a client has met with a caterer to discuss details of the event, he or she will typically expect the caterer to be responsible for the following:

♦ Planning a menu and possibly a decorating scheme

♦ Shopping for ingredients and supplies

♦ Preparing and cooking the food

♦ Setting up tables and serving areas

♦ Decorating the site according to the client's desires

♦ Serving the guests

♦ Cleaning up after the event

As a caterer, you may be asked to take care of additional services such as tending a bar or hiring a bartender, and arranging for flowers, music, and/or a photographer. Whether or not you are willing to handle these "extras" is a decision you must make when first starting your business.

Please Cater Our...

Unless you plan to specialize in catering for a particular type of function, you should be prepared to provide services and menus for a variety of meals, including breakfast, brunch, lunch, tea, and dinner. The following are examples of events typically catered by an outside firm:

- Office parties
- Cocktail receptions
- Theme parties
- Open houses
- Intimate meals for two to ten
- Fundraisers
- Corporate functions
- Church socials
- Cultural events
- Birthday and anniversary celebrations
- Graduation parties
- Bar Mitzvahs
- Bridal and baby showers
- Wedding receptions

There are two major categories of catering service. In *off-premise* catering, the food is prepared ahead of time and delivered to the client's event. *On-site* catering involves bringing the food and supplies to a prearranged location (such as a banquet room, social hall, or a private home), and preparing the food there.

As a caterer, you are likely to run across both of these situations and should be ready to work accordingly, unless zoning restrictions prohibit the use of your home kitchen as a base for operation. However, even in on-site catering, it is customary for the caterer to handle much of the preparation ahead of time. Whenever possible, plan on preparing desserts, appetizers, and raw vegetables before going to the site of the event.

Qualifications for Catering

Though no special training is required to start a successful catering business, the potential caterer should at the very least enjoy working with food, and have some experience preparing and serving it. A solid understanding of weights, measures, and the basics of food preparation are essential to creating the menus that are currently in demand. Most caterers will tell you that today's clientele expects not just potato puffs and Chicken Cordon Bleu, but rather the more sophisticated and creative fare they have become accustomed to in nouvelle and ethnic restaurants.

Some caterers held jobs as restaurant cooks before expanding into a into an independent catering venture. Others, however, have parlayed their experience from years of planning and preparing family meals into a profitable business. Whether you are looking for a basic cooking class or just want to expand your repertoire of recipes, check the offerings of local colleges, universities, community centers, and adult education institutions. Their classes are generally comprehensive and inexpensive.

In recent years, clients have become more sophisticated and discerning about their food choices. The interest in gourmet cooking can actually make your job as a caterer more interesting and fun. Many caterers claim that seeking out and trying new recipes and ideas is one of the most rewarding aspects of the business!

Attempt the impossible in order to improve your work.
Bette Davis

Culinary magazines and cookbooks will help you keep up with food trends. Guests of catered events expect to find food that is not only delicious, but also *different*. American Nouvelle cuisine—a light and healthy option—has been popularized in recent years, as have various ethnic foods such as Thai, Southwestern, and Cajun cuisine. Also, the interest in vegetarian and low-fat food has never been stronger. Expand your repertoire of recipes by experimenting with these types of food, and trying out recipes on friends and family.

The presentation of food is as important as the taste. Now more than ever, caterers are providing clients with food as art—

from sculpted melons to goose-shaped pâté to tri-color appetizers. At the very least, the food should be arranged and presented so that every item looks appetizing and complements the other items on the menu. Cookbooks and magazines are helpful resources for presentation ideas, as are classes and hands-on seminars.

A working knowledge of etiquette and traditional table arrangements and settings is an essential skill for any caterer. Clients will expect you to know the difference between setting up a bridal rehearsal dinner and preparing for a formal corporate function. They will also expect you and your staff to perform whatever services are appropriate to the situation. Check your local library for books on etiquette and table arrangements and settings. Amy Vanderbilt and Emily Post are considered authorities on traditional etiquette, and Miss Manners (Judith Martin) presents a humorous modern approach.

> *Organize! Don't agonize.*
>
> Florynce Kennedy

Planning and organization are key to successful catering. Each catered event is a separate and unique production, and the various components—shopping, food preparation, equipment rental, and hundreds of details—must be smoothly orchestrated.

Most caterers use wall charts, planning worksheets, and job envelopes to stay on track. Good planning and organization will also help you maintain your composure and calmly deal with any last-minute crises.

A good caterer must be willing to work hard and be able to cope with the long hours involved in planning and executing an event. During holidays and weekends, some caterers work ten- to fifteen-hour days. Although the business is relatively easy and inexpensive to start, the enterprising caterer needs drive and determination and good health to become and remain successful.

The social skills of a caterer are as important as his or her cooking and organizational skills. The role ranges from providing moral support to nervous hosts to discussing culinary trends with guests to maintaining a sophisticated and professional demeanor. Regardless of the type of event, the caterer's ability to adapt to the mood and occasion will work to his or her advantage.

Neatness counts. Prospective clients may want to inspect your equipment, food containers, and, if you work off-premise, your preparation facilities. Make it a point to operate your kitchen and your business as if at any moment you could be inspected.

Your cooking equipment, workspace, and serving pieces must be kept sanitary, and you and your staff should always be clean and well-groomed. No one wants to accept food from someone with hair in their eyes or a half-pound of flour sprinkled down the front of their uniform. Make sure your entire catering operation presents a professional image at all times.

A Few More Points

Other suggestions for maintaining a successful business are as follows:

♦ Be on time (or, even better, 15 minutes early).

♦ Maintain a sense of humor when situations (or pressured clients) get out-of-hand.

♦ Believe in your ability to get the job done.

♦ Market yourself and your skill to potential clients.

♦ Stay within your budget and projected profit margin for each event you cater.

4

OPERATIONS

Keeping Track of Details

The contract has been signed, the details worked out, and you have your 50 percent deposit in hand. Now you're ready to begin putting the job together.

Each catering job involves so many details that it is easy to become frustrated or to forget something until the last minute. You can avoid undue stress by employing some simple planning techniques.

The greater the difficulty, the more glory there is in surmounting it. Skillful pilots gain their reputations from storms and tempests.

Anonymous

Job Envelopes

The easiest method of keeping track of the paperwork involved in catering is to create a job envelope for each job. A job envelope is a 9 x 12-inch manila envelope that holds receipts for food and supplies, a copy of the signed contract, the menu to be served, and any correspondence or notes about conversations with the client.

On the outside of each job envelope, written directly on the envelope or on a preprinted card, include the following information:

Job Envelope Details

◆ Client name, address and phone number

◆ Event or occasion

◆ Date, time and location of function

◆ Number of guests

◆ Quoted cost per contract

◆ Deposit received (amount and date)

◆ Number of servers needed

◆ Extras such as wine, liquor, flowers, music, chinaware, and decorations

◆ Notes about special menu considerations or other specifics

Preparing for Peak Periods

Your ability to be organized is essential to your success as a caterer, but takes on heightened importance during the typically busy months of May and June (wedding receptions and graduations) and November and December (holiday parties).

Catering Tip

Maintain the highest standards possible in your food preparation, in presentation, and in service to ensure a solid position in the market. *Never sacrifice quality as a means of saving time.*

Take advantage of the quiet, slow days to prepare for the busy catering seasons by creating checklists, forms and other useful job aids. The following forms should be kept on hand at all times:

♦ Food requirement lists for each menu item

♦ Purchase orders for food and supplies

♦ Job tickets to outline what tasks need to be done and when

♦ Sample floor plans to indicate table and serving station arrangements and access to kitchen

♦ Cost sheets for breaking down all expenses

♦ Invoices

♦ Packing slips listing every item that must be taken to the site

Maintaining precise and current records will make year-end book-keeping functions go smoothly. Ask your accountant and the trade associations provided in the appendix for additional forms to make your work flow smoothly and efficiently.

Tasks should be broken down specifically by job and day. For a job starting Saturday at 4 p.m., a job ticket for the preceding days might look like this:

Tuesday	*Thursday*	*Friday*
Order Food	Cook Chicken	Make Salads
Hire Staff	Rent Supplies	Pack Dishes

YOUR CATERING COMPANY
1 Main Street 555-5555
Contract for Catering Services

Client Name _____

Name of Organization _____

Address _____

Phone (Home) _____ (Work) _____

Occasion _____

Type of Service _____

Date _____ Day _____ Time _____

Location _____

Number of Guests _____ Price Per Person _____

Total Amount _____ Method of Payment _____

Deposit Amount _____ Date Received _____

MENU _____

EXTRAS _____

NOTES _____

Signed By _____

Title _____ Date _____

*If cancellation is made one week prior to the event date indicated above, 50% of the deposit will be returned. Caterer retains the right to keep 100% of the deposit if cancellation is made after that time, except in the case of extreme emergencies, in which case, 50% will be returned.

Initials _____

Ten Tips for Success

You will be well on your way to success within a short time if you follow these guidelines suggested by caterers around the country.

1. Take the time to develop exciting menus for various occasions. Seek out recipes in magazines and books, and ask friends to share their favorites.

2. Decide on your primary market (for example, private individuals, businesses, or charitable organizations), and target your promotional efforts accordingly. One key to successful promotion is repetition; though much of your business will come through word-of-mouth advertising, an ongoing marketing campaign is essential.

3. To ensure a good reputation, maintain the highest standards possible in everything you do. Never sacrifice quality in either food preparation or service.

4. Plan ahead. Allow yourself plenty of time to handle the multitude of tasks involved in each catering job.

5. When hiring employees, discuss your standards, safety guidelines, and sanitation rules. Let potential workers know what will be expected of them.

6. Interview potential employees for full-time and part-time work even when you aren't actively hiring. This will allow you to have a large pool of workers to choose from when you need them. Students, homemakers, retirees, and waitpersons may have cooking and/or serving experience as well as the flexibility to work weekends and evenings.

7. In selecting ingredients for your menus, buy only the best. The extra expense can be incorporated into your price schedules. Clients will not mind paying a premium when they know you consistently provide them with the finest and freshest ingredients available.

8. Always be on time, or even a few minutes early. Your clients are counting on you to deliver, so never give them a reason to worry.

9. Treat each client as your *only* client. Catering is a very personal service. By going out of your way to make your clients feel important, you are assuring yourself and your business of a great reputation and a busy future.

10. Be creative in your cooking. A few clients will request standard fare, but most will expect you to provide unique selections. Keep abreast of culinary trends and incorporate new dishes into your menu selections as soon as you feel comfortable preparing them. Learn to be creative and innovative with garnishes, arrangement of food on plates, color combination, and other food presentation opportunities.

Notes

Key Points

Personal Thoughts

Additional Research

5

EQUIPMENT AND SUPPLIES

Your Computer System

It is not essential that your catering business be computerized in the beginning, but it is advisable. Keeping records, menus, floor plans, and correspondence on the computer will help you run the business efficiently and professionally.

In choosing your computer, the following criteria should be considered: the speed of the overall system and, related to this, the on-board (resident) software that drives the computer and its compatibility with other software packages that you may need down the road.

In addition, you'll want to check the system's upgrade capability (the ease with which you can upgrade components when the manufacturer offers new or revised product lines) and the system's overall compatibility with hardware offered by various competing manufacturers.

Once you've decided on your business applications and software needs, the next step is buying the hardware. Hardware comprises not only the computer (central processing unit or CPU, monitor, mouse, and keyboard), but also peripherals (printers, modems, etc.) and add-ons (such as fax and graphics boards).

In a constantly changing computer market, your best bets include reading the appropriate computer journals, calling manufacturers' customer service departments, and—most important—comparison shopping.

Hardware prices can vary widely from store to store, so it literally pays to shop around. Talk to a variety of salespeople, but don't let them talk you into a purchase. It's your decision, and it's too important to let it be dictated by a commission-hungry pitchman. Take your time, then base your decision first on need, then on price. A low price is no bargain if you walk away with a computer whose memory or other functions are inadequate or—worse yet—incompatible with your software needs.

In selecting hardware, your main considerations center on

1. Current and future business applications

2. Software requirements

3. Necessary peripherals

4. Price

Term Warfare

The first challenge in hunting for hardware is surviving the initial cross fire of computer-speak. If you can master a few simple terms (and can type), you'll most likely master the computerized home environment.

First, a few basics. The core of a computer system is the central processing unit, which among other things interacts with software. Virtually all CPUs contain at least one floppy disk drive, designed for either 5.25" or 3.5" magnetic disks on which text, graphics, and additional data are stored. The main storage area, however, is the system's internal or "fixed" drive, also known as the hard disk, which offers increased storage capacity.

Storage capacity refers to the amount of data that can be saved and is measured in terms of bytes or characters (each alphabetic letter, number, or punctuation mark represents a character). Under one million characters, floppy-disk storage is measured in kilobytes, signified with a capital K: An 800K disk thus can store 800,000 characters. Storage of one-million-plus characters is

measure in megabytes, signified with a capital M or MB. A 30MB hard drive thus can store up to thirty million bytes of data.

In addition to storing data (broken down into files), floppy and hard drives store and load software, allowing immediate access to a variety of programs.

The second element in the computer system is the monitor, or screen, available either in monochrome (black and white) or color. If you will be doing a lot of graphics work, a color monitor is essential. A mouse or other pointer device is necessary for most of the applications you will be using. There is also the keyboard, with a layout similar to that of a typewriter. Placement of function keys and the touch or feel of the keyboard are the major differences between models.

Next, you must consider peripherals—most commonly the printer and modem. Printers come in three forms: dot matrix, ink jet, and laser.

Modems transmit and receive computer data over telephone lines, connecting you electronically with the outside world—whether a print shop down the street or a client in Europe.

Modems usually are categorized by their transmission (or baud) rate, measured in bits (characters) per second (bps). Baud rates are typically 9600, 14400, or 28800. Modems of 9600 baud and higher are recommended for long documents. The higher the baud rate, the faster the transmission time and thus the lower your phone bill, since transmission time is billed as telephone time. In addition, there is the fax modem, which turns your telephone into a data retrieval/transmission center.

A low price is no bargain if you walk away with a computer whose memory or other functions are inadequate or incompatible with your software.

Finding the Right System

The leading-edge computer market is divided into two segments: the Apple Macintosh and IBM compatibles, the latter now dominated by Windows—a graphical user interface similar to that

of the Macintosh. Here's where things get both interesting and a little confusing. The growth of desktop publishing has resulted in a flood of products, and it can be difficult to make your equipment choices. The choice does, however, essentially boil down to two general computer environments: the Apple Macintosh or Microsoft Windows for the IBM PC and its clones.

What makes one better or worse than the other? That decision must be left in the hands of consumers. Each camp has its loyal followers; you'll need to decide what system you personally like best. Here is some general comparative information about each system.

	Macintosh	Windows
Ease of Use	Better	
Ease of Learning New Software	Better	
Graphics Capabilities	Comparable	Comparable
Price of Hardware	Comparable	Comparable
Availability of Hardware	Comparable	Comparable
Availability and Cost of Service		Slightly better
Price of Software	Comparable	Comparable
Availability of Quality Software	Comparable	Comparable
Price of Peripherals		Slightly better
Availability of Peripherals	Comparable	Comparable
Compatibility With Other Businesses	Comparable	Comparable

Instead of outlining all of the available hardware (something that would fill the heftiest of computer magazines), we'll concentrate on the variables that you should consider prior to making a purchase decision.

Keep in mind, however, that you don't have to buy new. You can purchase good late-model systems through computer rental

stores (leasing with an option to buy), as well as through used computer outlets and private parties.

Computer Shopping Checklist

◆ Will the computer handle the software programs you've selected, as well as the programs you eventually may need?

◆ How much memory do the software programs require, and does the system need to be expanded to handle them?

◆ What will it cost to expand the system, if necessary?

◆ Is the storage capacity of the hard drive adequate?

◆ How much setup space is required for the computer, printer, and other equipment?

◆ Is the operating system a user-friendly one, with easy-to-use commands and a comprehensive instruction manual?

◆ What assistance or technical support does the hardware manufacturer provide?

◆ Is the monitor an adequate size and resolution for your needs?

◆ What does the basic system price include (monitor, additional software, etc.)?

◆ What are the terms and length of the warranty, and to what extent is labor included?

◆ What kind of supplemental service contract is available? What will it cost on a monthly or annual basis?

◆ Does the dealer offer ongoing support?

- ◆ What is the quality of printer output?

- ◆ How fast and loud is the printer?

- ◆ Is the dealer willing to put a quote in writing for comparison shopping?

- ◆ Is financing available through the manufacturer or dealer? At what interest rate?

- ◆ Is a leasing program available? Can you purchase the equipment at the end of the term? At what price?

Printers

Here we offer a quick roundup of the leading laser, dot-matrix, and ink-jet printers. Shop around for the best deal.

Laser. If you are planning to produce menus or invoices with high print quality, you'll need a laser printer, which produces camera-ready copy at a fraction of the price charged by typesetting houses.

Laser printers work on a principle similar to photocopiers. The image from the document stored in your computer is transferred to a drum by a laser beam. The drum then lays an electrostatic charge on the paper that attracts toner into the areas to be printed. The images are set in a series of minute dots that look like solid lines to the naked eye. Printer resolution is measured in dots per inch (dpi). The higher the resolution the sharper the image. Laser printer resolution is typically 300, 600, 1000, or 1200 dpi. Printers with higher resolution will generally cost more and print more slowly than their lower dpi counterparts.

Laser printers have become increasingly affordable in recent years, turning the home computer into a full-scale type and graphics center.

Dot matrix. These printers produce characters composed of hundreds of dots and are popular choices for the budget-conscious who don't require high-resolution printing capabilities.

Ink jet. These printers produce pages of text or graphics by spraying fine jets of ink on the paper to form characters made up

of many dozens of dark black dots. Ink-jet output is often confused with that of low-resolution laser printers. For this reason an ink-jet printer is a good compromise between the high resolution and high cost of lasers and the rough resolution and low cost of dot-matrix printers.

Laptops and Notebooks

These lightweight, battery-powered computers can be used as standalone systems or as add-ons to your home computer, in both cases providing system access at remote locations—from the back seat of a limo or from an aircraft at thirty thousand feet.

> *Base your hardware purchases on current and future applications, needed software, available peripherals, and, of course, price.*

CD-ROMs

This stands for compact disc read-only memory. It is important to remember that CD-ROMs do not replace hard drives and other storage media because you cannot save your own files to them. (Rewritable CD systems are available, but they are extremely expensive.) Instead, they are used as a means of storing huge amounts of ready-made data, including software applications. They are capable of storing 150,000 pages of text per CD as well as complex graphics and sounds. For this reason they are used to store everything from downloadable fonts to sixty-million-word dictionaries to encyclopedias that allow users to listen and view as well as read. CD-ROMs are standard equipment on a number of systems and are now available at an increasingly reasonable cost.

Additional Accessories

Surge suppressors prevent damage to your equipment when there is a fluctuation in voltage. Basically a long strip or box with several power outlets and an on/off switch, they are well worth the minimal investment of less than $50, especially if you live in an area where power spikes or surges are common. You should

note, however, that a surge suppressor will not protect unsaved data in the event of a power failure. For that you need an uninterruptible power supply (UPS). You should also be wary of power strips that are not surge protectors. They often look similar, but their only function is to increase the number of outlets. Some surge suppressors come with guarantees that reimburse you for equipment that is damaged by power surges while you are using the suppressor.

Computer and printer covers protect your equipment from dust, which can sneak into the disk drives and under the keys to create problems. They cost an average of $10 to $20 each.

Screen filters reduce glare from windows or lights that reflect off the computer screen and into your eyes, causing eyestrain and headaches. Although a lower level of light is required for computer input than when working with a typewriter or writing by hand, it's sometimes impossible to prevent glare from a window. For less than $25, you can buy an external mesh or plastic screen filter.

Disk storage boxes come in a variety of styles and sizes. Generally made of plastic, they not only allow you to keep your library of disks in one convenient place, they also help you protect the disks from electromagnetic fields, which can alter and even erase data from disks. Keep your disks in the box and keep the box at least three feet away from electronic equipment (such as telephones, calculators, TVs, and stereos).

Removable storage media. High-end work, especially involving graphics, requires manipulation of large amounts of data. Removable media accommodate the storage and transportation of large files. You will find this equipment indispensable if you must transport files that are too big to fit on floppy disks. There are several types of systems that vary in access speed, compatibility, and price per megabyte.

Shop Carefully

Again, we can't stress enough that it pays to shop carefully. Computer systems can range from below $1,000 to well over $5,000, with many of the lower-priced systems offering all the power and speed you'll need. It's very easy to overspend on

technology that you don't really require and that is available at a lower price on less expensive models.

Read the leading hardware and software computer magazines and comparison shop at a variety of stores. Also, as mentioned earlier, there's a good chance you'll be able to find a perfectly good previously owned system at a very reasonable price, particularly in light of recent hardware upgrades inducing users to trade up. Check the classifieds and local computer users groups for good purchase opportunities.

Mail Order

The same principle applies with mail-order computer houses that advertise in computer magazines. It is possible to save hundreds of dollars buying brand-new systems from mail-order outlets, and you can also buy components.

In either case, do some preliminary research before buying. To the extent possible, know what you're getting.

Financing and Leasing

Many of the major computer manufacturers offer their own financing packages, and major computer hardware stores do as well. Of course, monthly payments are required and, in some instances, interest rates may be above those you could obtain through a personal or business loan. Here, too, it pays to comparison shop to be sure you get the best financing available.

Leasing can be an advantage, since it offers the opportunity to trade in one computer on an upgraded model down the line. You may also have the option of buying the hardware at the end of the term for a preset price. Leasing is discussed in more detail at the end of this chapter.

Backup Service and Support

You need to be aware of things that *can* go wrong, so when they *do* go wrong, you have at least some idea of what your options are. The good thing about computer equipment is that most routine problems can be avoided by careful operation and preventive maintenance. If you have no background in computers, you will

definitely need to read up on the equipment's operating parameters and tips for the best care possible. Local computer dealers can suggest books for your particular computer.

To protect yourself from the worst twists of Murphy's Law, plan on covering yourself with these two things:

1. A data backup system

2. Equipment insurance

Why should you back up your data? Because if you don't, and your hard disk is damaged somehow, there's a good chance you'll never see those data again. Here's a case in point that's very close to home: The computer that was being used to write this book was on when a power failure occurred. For reasons unclear even to the computer's manufacturer, the hard drive froze up and wouldn't work. Approximately twenty-five megabytes of data on the drive were lost forever because this writer had forgotten to back up the text on to floppy disks on a regular basis. The lesson is that computers are only machines; they don't think. Be sure you always back up data.

For insurance purposes, assume that you'll be working out of your home initially. You may already have coverage through your homeowner's policy. If you rent, ask your insurance agent about a renter's policy that covers the contents of your home against theft and damage; likewise if you rent an office. There are a number of ways to cover the equipment without having to take out a special policy—ask your agent. But above all, *make sure the equipment is insured in some way.*

As with any electronic device, computers break down and will need to be repaired. This can be costly, not only for parts and service but also in lost production time. Therefore, be sure any new system you're planning to buy has a good warranty and has a service contract available. (In some cases, used computer stores also offer limited warranties, so be sure to ask when shopping the market.)

New system warranties vary greatly in duration. Any warranty or service contract should cover both parts and labor. One drawback, no matter how good the warranty, is that you'll be required to ship the computer to the service center, perhaps at your

own expense. If possible, try to have the dealer sign a statement covering the cost of shipping if the system needs service within the warranty period. Also, ask whether loaners are provided while your system is being repaired.

Service or maintenance contracts may seem like a heavy expense when you've just laid out hundreds and perhaps thousands of dollars on a new system. However, in the event that you need to have major work done—replacing a disk drive, for example—you'll be thankful you made the investment.

General Office Equipment

Office needs in this business are minimal and paperwork can be taken care of very easily, especially if you start maintaining good records from the beginning. As the business grows, however, your administrative duties will increase. More jobs will be booked, calling for the preparation of contracts, lists, menus, and employee information.

When your budget warrants it, start investigating prices for the following equipment and supplies that you will eventually need to handle your administrative responsibilities efficiently.

♦ Desk

♦ Chair

♦ Typewriter

♦ Calculator

♦ Index card file

♦ Desk-top organizer

♦ Weekly planning calendar

♦ Monthly planning calendar

♦ File cabinet

♦ Shelves for etiquette & cookbooks

♦ Invoices

♦ Letterhead stationery

♦ Envelopes

♦ Stamps

♦ Pens & pencils

♦ Paper clips

♦ Stapler

♦ Specific business forms

Kitchen Supplies and Equipment

Your first purchasing priority should be the "tools of the trade"—supplies and equipment required to prepare and serve food to clients and their guests. The ready-for-anything caterer's kitchen will include the following items:

In the Kitchen

- Measuring cups and spoons
- Cooking utensils (spatulas, etc.)
- Baking dishes
- Soup pot
- Pots & pans (variety)
- Cookbooks
- Recipe file
- Food grinder
- Cutting boards
- Accessories, i.e., garlic press
- Refrigerator
- Freezer
- Stove with oven
- Mixer
- Blender
- Food processor
- Microwave
- Kitchen knives
- Can opener
- Dishwasher
- Sink with garbage disposal
- Aprons
- Ice maker
- Food preparation tables
- Storage boxes and containers
- Transport cases on casters
- Potholders
- Dish cloths
- Cleaning supplies
- Garbage bags
- Sponges
- First-aid kit

On the Table

Unless you plan to use clients' dishes and silverware for place settings and serving, prepare to invest in the following pieces (service for 50 is optimum):

◆ Dessert plates

◆ Dinner plates

◆ Luncheon plates

◆ Salad plates

◆ Bread plates

◆ Soup bowls

◆ Cups with saucers

◆ Sugar and creamer

◆ Glasses, including wine, water, juice, parfait, champagne, etc.

◆ Cutlery: forks—dinner, salad, fish, and dessert
knives—dinner, luncheon, spreader
spoons—soup, tea, ice tea, and table

Required for Serving

◆ Tea pot (or Samovar)

◆ Coffee urn

◆ Doilies

◆ Tablecloths (fabric)

◆ Placemats (fabric)

◆ Napkins (fabric and paper)

◆ Cocktail napkins (paper)

◆ Buffet cloths

◆ Silver trays

◆ Chafing dishes

◆ Platters

◆ Large bowls

◆ Heating unit/tray

◆ Ice buckets

◆ Ice chest

◆ Kitchen and bar trays

- ◆ Candelabra candles and holders
- ◆ Pitchers—water and coffee
- ◆ Creamers and sugar bowls
- ◆ Bread baskets
- ◆ Butter dishes
- ◆ Salt and pepper shakers
- ◆ Relish trays

- ◆ Flower vases
- ◆ Ashtrays
- ◆ Matches
- ◆ Toothpicks
- ◆ Corkscrew
- ◆ After-dinner mints
- ◆ Folding tables and chairs
- ◆ Serving uniforms

The majority of items listed above, including linens and table settings, can be rented from major party or equipment rental companies listed in the Yellow Pages. Most rental companies guarantee delivery of clean and ready-to-go items at a relatively low cost. What's more, they will deliver directly to the site of the catered event. Some rental companies will even pick up the dirty dishes after the event (for an additional fee, of course), cutting *your* clean-up time by at least half.

Renting on a per-event basis also eliminates the need for roomy storage areas and saves the time spent packing and unpacking these items. Obtain prices and an outline of specific responsibilities from several rental companies in your area before making your first bid for a catering job.

Buying Equipment and Supplies

There is almost no reason to pay high prices for office and working supplies. Office supply discount stores and wholesale catalogs sell everything needed to outfit your office for around 50 percent of standard retail prices. By shopping smartly, you can purchase *all* of the office necessities listed previously for under $300.

You can also find reasonably priced kitchen supplies such as spatulas, cooking spoons, pots and pans, small equipment, and accessories at department stores such as Kmart. For bigger items,

check restaurant equipment warehouses. By shopping carefully at both types of suppliers, you can spend less than $400 for a basic stock of cooking utensils, baking dishes, pots and pans, and fancy accessories.

You can find many of the items you need in your kitchen cupboards and drawers, and you may be able to borrow others from friends or family. Watch the classified ads in the newspaper for liquidation sales of businesses and restaurants that are closing. Finally, if you don't mind rummaging through other people's belongings, you can find great bargains on supplies at swap meets, garage sales, and thrift shops.

New or Used?

Before investing money, do your homework. Talk with other business owners to find out which brand of equipment they use and why they prefer it over other choices on the market. This will help you make the best decision based on your needs and budget.

Also, talk with independent dealers who carry a broad line of similar types of equipment. They can give you insights on maintenance, longevity, service contracts, and prices.

They will also be able to tell you when to expect a drop in price for the item you are interested in, although you can count on seeing sales on major equipment such as computers and other big-ticket items at store openings and during special sales.

Cash or Credit?

Unless you are planning to pay cash for an equipment purchase, you will either make a down payment and set up a payment schedule with the dealer or take out a loan with the bank. Shop around to determine whether or not a dealer is willing to handle the financing at a lower rate than the bank.

Although this method is a less effective way of establishing your credit, it will serve to get the business going. Another advantage is that if you should find yourself in a tight cash-flow situation at any time, a private dealer/lender with whom you have a personal relationship is much more likely to be flexible...without charging you a penalty for a late payment.

Looking for Bargains

There are many ways to save money buying equipment and supplies, generally through third-party vendors and mail-order sources. Apple and IBM equipment is sold only through authorized dealers, while IBM clones and third-party peripherals are available everywhere from small stores to mail-order businesses run by electronics whizzes who create their own computers and accessories.

A word of caution here: You need reliable equipment that is backed up by warranty. Whatever your decision on brand, make sure you are protected with a company that stands behind what it sells.

Shopping around is the only way to get the best deal on equipment and software. If you live in a small town, buy a newspaper for the nearest big city and look for computer ads.

Buying Used Equipment

When buying used equipment from a dealer, the chances of it being in working condition are generally pretty good. Dealers have a reputation to uphold and will stand behind their merchandise, especially if they are firmly established in the community. There are, however, several ways you can scout around to ensure that the one you decide to work with is reputable.

- ◆ Find a store with membership in the local chamber of commerce. Although this is not an iron-clad guarantee, it does indicate the store owner's interest in following business standards established within the community.

- ◆ If the dealer also sells new equipment, it is highly likely that much of the used equipment has been traded in by people who are upgrading. You may be able to get an excellent deal on an item that has been carefully maintained by the former owner.

- ◆ If there is a service department on the premises, you can be assured that used equipment has been reconditioned before being put on sale. It also increases your chances of getting fast, inexpensive, and reliable service if needed at a later date.

♦ Used equipment dealers realize that it is not always easy to find a buyer and should be willing to work with you. Shopping around will give you an idea of average prices and will give you the information you need to negotiate. If the dealer won't work with you, keep looking.

♦ Know the terms of the warranty. Even used equipment should be covered for a short time for parts and labor, especially if it has been overhauled or reconditioned.

♦ Ask the dealer if he or she is willing to agree to offer a trade-in allowance on the item you are buying when you decide to upgrade. Of course there will be stipulations based on wear and tear and time; however, the dealer should be willing to consider it.

♦ Contact your local Better Business Bureau to see if any complaints have been made about the dealer.

Buyer Beware

There are other ways to find and buy used equipment, but it falls into the realm of "buyer beware." If you choose to deal with private parties through the classified ads or with auctioneers selling off the inventory of a bankrupt business, you must be willing to take a chance. Although the prices will be easy on your budget, the cost of repairing a malfunctioning machine could result in a long-term drain on your profits.

Ask a private party how long they have owned the equipment, why it is being sold, and if there are any repair bills that you can look at.

This is not to say that there aren't good opportunities out there. The secret is to know what you are looking for and to have a good idea of how it should work. Do your research by visiting with reliable used-equipment dealers before you start looking.

Ask a private party how long they have owned the equipment, why it is being sold, and if there are any repair bills that you can look at. Trust your intuition in this kind of situation; if the party seems truly interested in providing you with as much

information as possible, chances are the equipment is as claimed. If you're told it needs a new part, for example, find out what the replacement part costs and ask if that amount could be deducted from the selling price.

When you go to see the equipment, make sure it runs. Test it out, if possible, and measure it to make sure it will fit into the space you have available. Also, see whether you can move it yourself or will have to arrange transportation.

Before buying the equipment try to find out if there is a servicing outlet nearby or if you must send away for parts, which can be time-consuming and costly, especially when it comes to older models.

Occasionally you will run across an individual who is making payments on a piece of equipment still under warranty. This can be a great deal for you since he or she will probably accept a small amount of cash and let you take over the payments. Be sure to transfer ownership in writing to prevent complications if you need service under the warranty.

Auctions

Auctions are an excellent way to get equipment and supplies at good prices. Watch the business and classified sections of the newspaper for ads about upcoming auctions. The ad will include dates, the reason for the auction (liquidation or bankruptcy), location, time, and a partial list of items. In most cases there will be a preview, enabling potential buyers to view the merchandise before the bidding begins. Take advantage of the preview to inspect and select the equipment you want to bid on. A fee will be required for a bidder registration number, which is held up when you make a bid so the auctioneer's spotters know who has purchased a particular item.

There are two rules to remember at auctions:

1. Cash or a personal check for the full purchase amount must be paid on the day of the auction.

2. Don't move your hands or make significant gestures during bidding or you might find that you have purchased something you didn't want.

Leasing Equipment

Leasing is defined as a long-term agreement between two parties for the use of a specific item. The person who leases is known as the lessee, while the owner of the item is referred to as the lessor.

Despite the fact that you do not own the equipment when you lease, and so cannot take advantage of depreciation on it for tax purposes, there are still many benefits for the beginning business owner.

Leasing lets you try out a piece of equipment for a given period of time to determine if it is the best product for your needs. Although you are locked in to the terms of the lease, most lessors are flexible.

Know What You Need

Of course, the best way to enter into a lease is to be absolutely clear about what you expect the equipment to do for you. The service representative from the leasing company is well-versed in tailoring equipment to the customer, so do not hesitate to ask questions about capabilities.

Most lessors offer good maintenance contracts, as they want to protect their equipment. Check to see what parts and/or labor are covered before signing the lease. The lessor should also be willing to provide technical advice at no charge, may be willing to offer installation and setup of the equipment, and may also provide training, if required.

Payments can be arranged to fit your budgetary needs on a monthly, semiannual, or annual basis. This gives you the freedom to schedule payments for peak cash-flow periods. You can also negotiate the rates and length of the lease to keep monthly operating expenses at a minimum.

Conditional Sales Agreement

Under the provisions of a conditional sales agreement, you become the owner of the leased goods from the agreement date. At the end of the lease period, you are required to purchase the item for a preestablished price. This is often referred to as a balloon payment and should be agreed upon by you and the lessor prior to your signing the lease.

The conditional sales agreement, unlike most other leasing contracts, gives you the tax advantage of claiming depreciation on equipment. Depreciation refers to the decrease in the value of an asset because of wear and tear over a period of time.

You are entitled to deduct depreciation from your income tax based on the value when new, the estimated life of the item, and the value at the end of that estimated life. It is best to work with your accountant on determining depreciation of fixed assets.

There is seldom a down payment, other than the first month's lease amount, required on a leased item, since leasing is generally 100 percent financed for the terms of the agreement. This frees your start-up or working capital for other uses.

True Lease Agreements

You can write off lease payments on your income tax, but only if you have a true lease contract. Under a true lease, the lessor owns the equipment at all times during the contract period. If you decided, at the end of the lease, that you wanted to buy the equipment, you would have to pay whatever purchase price was decided by the lessor.

Financial Lease

The financial lease covers a period that does not extend beyond the estimated life of the equipment. Payments must be made as stipulated on the date due and made consistently to the end of the lease. It usually puts the responsibility and cost of maintenance on the lessee.

Operating Lease

The operating lease generally requires the lessor to handle maintenance of the equipment. It offers the option of canceling the lease, but only if a cancellation clause has been included at the negotiating stage.

The most important aspects of leasing are the terms outlined in the formal lease. Have the lessor draw up a proposal for you, based on everything you have discussed in an initial meeting. If you have any trouble understanding the terms of the proposal,

have your accountant review it with you. In fact, it is a definite advantage to have the final lease agreement checked by your attorney or accountant before you sign it.

Your Lease Agreement

Your lease agreement should include

- ♦ The length of the contract in months or years
- ♦ The rate you are to be charged, which is usually a percentage of the total purchase price computed on a monthly rate
- ♦ Your payment schedule
- ♦ A purchase option, if applicable, at the end of the lease
- ♦ A renewal option, if applicable, which allows you to carry the lease over for an additional period of time
- ♦ A cancellation agreement in the event you want or need to cancel the lease
- ♦ Maintenance stipulations (who pays for parts and labor)
- ♦ Substitution options if updated equipment is introduced and you want to take advantage of improvements
- ♦ Any provisions particular to the lease, including tax allowances for depreciation, insurance liability in case of loss or damage, and your responsibilities in reporting a move or other major change

Whether you decide to borrow, buy new equipment, find good used equipment, or lease, be sure to get exactly what you need to keep costs to a minimum. This is especially important during the early stages of your business when cash is bound to be tight. You can always upgrade or add to your equipment inventory as profits increase.

Do You Need a Delivery Vehicle?

Even when you do all the cooking at the site of the function, you will undoubtedly have to transport some food and equipment to

the site. For this reason, a station wagon or van will be an invaluable asset to your business.

As with equipment requirements, it isn't necessary to buy a new, fully outfitted vehicle (which will cost from $20,000 to $40,000, depending on the size and extras). Consider both passenger vans and cargo vans while shopping for a vehicle. One caterer tells the story of purchasing a non-operational, dilapidated van that he spotted in a yard by the freeway for $200. He towed it home, invited a couple of mechanically inclined friends over on a Saturday and together they had the vehicle operational within a few hours.

> *The greatest inspiration is a challenge to attempt the impossible.*
>
> A. Michelson

Another group of friends helped him sand the exterior and strip the interior. After a $250 paint job and the addition of several homemade cabinets, he owned a reliable, attractive vehicle for his Party Squad Catering Company.

Careful shopping through classified ads, auto shopper guides, and used car dealers can lead to a sound late-model van or station wagon for between $2,000 and $5,000. You may want to consider leasing, but keep in mind that the lease for a six-passenger van with no back seats ranges from $249 to $375 per month. This expense can be prohibitive in the early stages of establishing a business. Before making the decision to lease or buy, discuss the matter with your accountant, and review the expendable capital and tax implications of both options.

Notes

Key Points

Personal Thoughts

Additional Research

6

START-UP BASICS

Having decided that you are ready and able to accept the challenge of starting your own business, it is necessary to take a look at your overall financial picture. Even if you have a healthy savings account, or feel you can start your business with a minimal capital investment, diagnosing your personal financial situation will help you determine ongoing expenses.

The easiest way to estimate exactly how much money you will need to get your business started and to cover expenses, including personal living expenses for the first six months, is to prepare a *Cash Flow Statement* and a *Projected Expense Statement*. Samples are provided in this chapter.

Preparing the Projected Expense Statement will give you a fairly accurate picture of what it will cost to open the doors and will indicate how much income you must generate to realize a profit. Another advantage of creating these charts early in the game is that two of the required documents will already be prepared when you want to explore funding options; then you will only need to update them.

The first step in examining your financial situation is to ask yourself the following questions:

1. Do I generally pay my bills on time or do I wait until my creditors start sending me collection notices?

2. Have I regularly reconciled my bank statement so I know how much money I have in my checking account at any given time?

3. Is my philosophy "If I've got it, I spend it" or do I carefully plan how I am going to use my income?

4. Have I ever developed a personal budget so I know how much money is coming in, how much is going out, and what I have left over?

These are important aspects of your financial personality that will be helpful to understand when running your business. As your business and subsequent involvement with financial matters grow, it will be vital that you have a handle on your philosophy about money. And there is no time like in the beginning, when your business concept is being formed, to start learning.

The Cash Flow Statement

Use the Cash Flow Statement at the end of this chapter to determine your personal living expenses for the past three to six months to help you gauge what you will need to survive during the early stages of your business.

The easiest way to complete the statement is to use your checkbook register or sales receipts as research tools. If your expenses are relatively consistent from month to month, you should be able to get an overview by analyzing one month. A more accurate picture will emerge if you break down income and expenses for three to six months to account for periodic payments, such as taxes, insurance, and seasonal spending.

Using the samples provided, fill in the amounts in each category from your checkbook register or receipts. Use a separate sheet for every month that you are analyzing. For miscellaneous spending, a standard calculation is 5 percent of monthly income. Add up each month's expenses, total them all, and then divide that figure by the number of months you are analyzing. This will give you an average monthly expense figure.

Follow the same procedure for income. You can then subtract your expenses from your income to see where you stand. If you have computed your figures accurately, you might run across a few surprises. It isn't unusual to discover that we spend more money than we realize, often on unnecessary purchases. You may be able to see some areas where you can cut back.

The main points, however, are that you now know

1. How much or whether you can afford to invest your own money in your new business

2. What it costs for you to live comfortably, which will help you set income goals for the business

A six-month cost projection will be a good indicator not only of expenses near-term, but the kinds of profits you can expect as the business gets underway.

Start-up Costs

Every business owner has specific standards about how he or she wants to run the operation. One person may feel perfectly comfortable waiting to order business cards until there is a profit. Another wouldn't dream of opening the doors without cards, brochures, and letterhead already printed.

You will have your own ideas about what you need before opening your business. Then you must find out what it will cost and, if at all possible, prepare the Start-up Costs Worksheet at the end of this chapter.

It is also advisable to figure how much it will cost to run the business for three to six months, using the sample Projected Expense Statement. A six-month projection should give you the opportunity to determine your profits down the line.

Preparing the Start-up Costs Worksheet and Projected Expense Statement involves conducting some research. For example, to estimate the cost of business cards or letterhead stationery, contact several printers or copy shops in your area and obtain quotes. Call the local newspaper for prices on different types of ads, including display and classified.

An insurance agent will be able to give you an estimate on liability coverage. Check with the telephone company for information and rates on installing a phone line.

You can also start to shop around to find the best prices on office supplies, equipment, and materials to conduct business.

After you have completed your research, incorporate the information on the blank charts. Obviously, some of your figures, such as those for telephone expenses, will be guesstimated. However, the final figure will give you a good idea of start-up and operational costs for the first six months.

Utilizing the same theory, you can develop a *Projected Income Statement* (worksheet not provided), drawing from industry figures available through your trade association or other research sources. This would include all income realized from cash sales, collection on outstanding invoices, credit card sales, and miscellaneous income. By subtracting your total expenses from total income, you will get a clear picture of projected profit or loss.

All of these statements will be requested by loan officers, venture capitalists, and the Small Business Administration if and when you apply for a loan. This kind of paperwork is required to ensure that you have basic business knowledge, a commendable track record, and are serious about your venture. You will also be required to fill out a personal financial statement, available through the lending institution, especially if you are the sole owner or a general partner in the business.

Catering Business Start-up Costs
Based on Average Investment Using Home Kitchen

Basic cooking equipment *(including used oven and refrigerator, new food processor, meat slicer, and preparation table)*	$2,000.00
Kitchen supplies (utensils, baking dishes, etc.)	300.00
Office supplies and equipment	450.00
Licenses, permits, fictitious name statement	50.00
Initial inventory of food supplies	250.00
Utilities and telephone deposits	150.00
Legal and accounting start-up consultation	200.00
Insurance *(three months)*	500.00
Advertising and promotion	1,000.00
TOTAL	**$5,000.00**

For higher investment start-up in a commercial location, add:

Rent *(first and last month)*	$2,500.00
Leasehold improvements	1,500.00
Professional cooking/preparation equipment	10,000.00
Van or station wagon *(used, includes insurance)*	5,000.00
TOTAL	**$24,000.00**

Projected Expense Statement

Months:	1st	2nd	3rd	4th	5th	6th
Rent						
Utilities						
Telephone						
Insurance						
Professional services						
Taxes & licenses						
Advertising						
Office supplies						
Office equipment						
Inventory						
Business auto expense						
Travel expense						
Entertainment						
Dues & subscriptions						
Salaries						
Owner's draw						
Loan payments						
Interest payments						
Miscellaneous						
TOTALS						

Cash Flow Statement
Month of _____

Income		Expenses	
Wages	$_____	Rent or mortgage	$_____
Miscellaneous	$_____	Auto loan	$_____
		Gas & auto repairs	$_____
TOTAL	$_____	Auto insurance	$_____
		Life insurance	$_____
		Medical insurance	$_____
Savings	$_____	Homeowner's insurance	$_____
		Taxes	$_____
Credit Line	$_____	Loan payments	$_____
		Food: At home	$_____
		Food: Dining out	$_____
Home Equity	$_____	Telephone	$_____
		Utilities	$_____
		Household repairs, etc.	$_____
		Medical bills	$_____
		Credit card payments	$_____
		Interest expense	$_____
		Clothing/dry cleaning	$_____
		Travel	$_____
		Miscellaneous	$_____
		Savings	$_____
		TOTAL	$_____

Start-up Costs Worksheet

Furniture: Purchase price	$_____
Down payment required	$_____
Fixtures: Purchase price	_____
Down payment required	_____
Equipment: Purchase price	_____
Down payment required	_____
Installation & delivery costs	_____
Decorating & leasehold improvements	_____
Deposits: Utilities & rent	_____
Fees: Legal, accounting, consulting, etc.	_____
Licenses & permits	_____
Starting inventory	_____
Supplies	_____
Printing	_____
Initial advertising & promotion	_____
Miscellaneous	_____
Total Start-up Expense	$_____
Less Available Start-up Capital	$_____
Total Amount Needed	$_____

7

POTENTIAL CLIENTS

The increased demand for catering services is based primarily on social and economic changes such as the entrance of more women into the workplace and higher personal incomes. More and more hosts are realizing that having an event catered affords them the opportunity to relax and enjoy themselves.

Who are your potential customers? Take a moment to think about friends, relatives, and neighbors who have married, celebrated a birthday or anniversary, graduated from school, or retired from a job in the past year. Has anyone you know held a housewarming or had a reunion? Because nearly everyone celebrates these occasions at one time or another, there is no end to potential clients.

Knowledge itself can be described as awareness of unsolved problems.

Anonymous

Make a list of everyone you know. Even if some of the people on your list do not seem likely to hire a caterer, they may know someone else who *would* be interested in your catering service.

This list will serve you in both planning your initial business approach and in ongoing client recruiting. Start your list with the names of the following potential clients and contacts:

♦ Immediate family members

♦ Relatives and friends who live in the area

♦ Members of clubs and organizations in the area

♦ Acquaintances from work, school, church or social groups

♦ People from local retailers with whom you regularly do business

♦ Your mail carrier, landlord, and children's teachers

♦ Acquaintances through sports, recreation, or hobbies

♦ Your doctor, dentist, banker, plumber, babysitter, gardener, etc.

Talk to everyone on your list to find out whether they have a need for catering services or can give you the name of someone who might be a potential client. Hand out business cards and brochures and ask people to pass them along. Most friends and acquaintances will be happy to lend a hand in getting your business off the ground.

The Broader Market

Americans have become more appreciative in recent years of well-prepared, handsomely presented foods, but find that restaurants are too expensive when it comes to entertaining a large group. One reason the catering industry is booming is that the service eliminates much of the overhead expense one would pay at a restaurant.

In addition, people today have less time to plan and prepare meals, even though entertaining guests is as popular as ever.

Business Accounts Are Meat and Potatoes

The business world offers endless possibilities for catering, and accounts for as much as 65 percent of some caterers' business.

Chapter 22 offers advice on establishing a consistent public relations campaign for your catering business.

Once you have handled a few dinners for friends or relatives, you will be ready to approach commercial accounts. While a review of the local yellow pages will provide a wealth of potential accounts, following are a few tips to get you started:

♦ Owners of new businesses can benefit from an open house to introduce their product or service to the public.

♦ Art galleries often sponsor receptions for artists.

♦ Charitable organizations depend on fundraising events to attract capital.

♦ Real estate offices and insurance providers periodically host awards banquets for top salespeople.

♦ Theater companies hold cast parties on opening nights.

♦ Political and volunteer organizations regularly sponsor rallies and events.

♦ Social clubs and networking groups meet regularly.

♦ Small and large corporations hold seasonal parties, company picnics and management meetings.

Potential Customers

Friends and Relatives

Acquaintances and Service Providers

Business Contacts

8

A MARKETING OVERVIEW

Now that you have selected the kind of business you want to own, it is important to explore the need for it. A process known as *marketing research* will provide you with the information you need to develop your business, plan methods of distribution or promotion, and set prices that are tailored to the audience you hope to attract.

In addition, your marketing research will provide you with information that will help when you make decisions about a location, hours of operation, the specific types of services to offer, and how to gear your advertising.

Identifying Your Market

The process of identifying your audience may seem to be an extremely complex process; however, you can develop a perfectly workable and valuable marketing report by using the following guidelines and adapting them to your particular situation. Basically, there are five factors used to target the market.

Five Factors Used to Target Your Market

1. Population or demographics

2. Income

3. Competition

4. Product or service market match

5. Desire

1. ***Population.*** The number of households in the region you are considering for your business is crucial, as you must have a sufficient population base to produce the sales necessary to generate a profit. If the market for your product or service extends beyond your local region, it is important to identify the demographics for your target customers.

 Equally important is the circulation and age range of readers of the publications where you will be placing your advertising. If, for example, you are planning to sell products for infants, a publication whose readership is largely of retirement age would be inappropriate. It would, however, work in your favor if you were promoting health products or gift items. If you are selling a service such as catering, you might consider the food section of a newspaper or a journal of local businesses.

2. ***Income.*** Your potential customers must have the income to purchase goods and services. Consumers in the thirty-five to sixty-five age group generally have considerable income to spend on entertainment, household items, personal grooming, and sporting goods. This is not to discount the over-sixty-five age group, a large and growing segment of the nation's population which, depending on the region, has adequate discretionary income (money after taxes and necessities) to spend, or the eighteen to thirty-five age group, which is a desirable market for clothing, personal, and recreational items.

3. **Competition.** Competition shouldn't be a negative factor. Rather, it should spur you on to stretch your creativity by creating something brand new or creating a similar product or service that is superior to those being offered by the competition—through quality, selection, or price.

4. **Product or service market match.** Basically, this means that you must be able to attract those consumers whom you have the resources to serve. For example, if your idea of the perfect business involves national distribution of your patented weight-training equipment, you must reach an audience that is receptive and interested in bodybuilding through a carefully designed advertising campaign, and have the financing available to supply and ship the product.

5. **Desire.** Your objective is to match your product or service to the needs and desires of a particular group of consumers who will be responsive. It is often difficult to figure out exactly what your target market wants. However, through observation of what the competition is doing, it should be possible to recognize a need.

Market Research Techniques

Large corporations often have in-house marketing staffs who conduct extensive research on a continuing basis to ensure that the products or services being offered are in line with the marketplace. Obviously, this is an expensive and time-consuming process; one that you undoubtedly want to avoid.

Through several easy and inexpensive methods, you can find out everything you want to know about your potential market. But first you need to determine exactly what information you need. It might be population or economic trends, the number of new homes built locally within the last five years, or how many people are active in a particular hobby.

The nearest Census Bureau office and local chambers of commerce are consistently good sources for regional statistics. The reference librarian at the public library can steer you toward other data that will give you the specifics you seek.

The Small Business Administration (SBA) compiles extensive marketing information, in addition to material on operating procedures for specific types of businesses.

Check the *Encyclopedia of Associations* at the library to find the name and address of the advisory board for your industry. Trade boards can provide associates with marketing statistics, management tips, and a wealth of valuable information. Often it only takes a phone call to get more details than you could ever use.

Another excellent source of information on population, income, and sales figures is the annual survey of buying power published by *Sales and Marketing Management Magazine,* which breaks the information down by county and cities in the United States and should be available through the library.

Media Kits and Personal Contact

The advertising departments of local magazines and newspapers undoubtedly have a "media kit" available for potential advertisers, which they will gladly send you upon request. These packets contain a breakdown of their advertising rates and specifications, a description of why advertising with them is to your benefit and, most important, a profile of their readership. A friendly conversation with one of their salespeople should give you a wealth of data.

The merchants from whom you will be buying supplies, equipment, and products are another excellent source. They can give you a good rundown on trends, as well as an overview of current sales figures for their products. Since they are hoping you will eventually use them as a supplier for your business, they will be more than happy to give you free information.

It is, of course, often possible to gauge what the competition is doing and to glean information from them. There are two approaches when talking to people who are soon to be in direct competition. One is to be up-front and honest about your business plans and appeal to their sense of "industry spirit."

Surprisingly, you will find the direct approach works in the majority of cases as most people are genuinely interested in and supportive of others trying to make it in their field. It is better for everyone if "industry" standards are maintained and competitors

have a healthy rapport. And, except in extreme situations such as a very small community, there is generally enough business to go around. It shouldn't be difficult to capture your share of the market, especially if you can develop something unique to attract them.

On the other hand, if competitors are less than receptive, it may be necessary to do some detective work to get the information you want.

Focus Groups

If you really want to go into depth with your marketing study, you might consider gathering together a group of people (family members, a social or church group, or friends) for a focus session to determine if your product or service will match the needs of the prospective audience. This involves presenting your proposed business idea, with product samples if applicable, and creating a questionnaire that calls for specific answers from the members of the group.

Referral Discounts

Here's a way to boost your income that will make your clients happy to promote the business. Offer clients who provide you with the name of a potential customer (or who have someone call you) a discount on billing. If it results in a job, give a ten percent discount to the referring party.

This method is often used by companies when they are testing new products and, in fact, there are private companies that do nothing but put focus groups together and set up testing sites in stores, in shopping malls, and on street corners to obtain spontaneous and objective input from potential consumers.

The questions you would want to include on your survey would cover such aspects as how often members of the focus group have used a similar service or product in the past, what they liked

about it, what they found to be unsatisfactory, how they feel it could have been improved, whether they would be willing to try another, and vital statistics such as their age, income, and any specifics that relate to your proposed business.

With the catering business, the questions might include a breakdown of the top three reasons people in your focus group would consider using a service like yours, what type of catering they would desire, and what *additional* services they would like to see offered. This kind of information will give you an immediate edge on the competition when you are ready to start advertising.

Analyzing Your Research

The bottom line in conducting your research is that you want to zero in on information that provides insights on the potential for your business idea before you invest time, money, and energy in setting it up.

If, for example, you were considering starting your business in a small community, and your focus group information indicated that only 10 percent of the local residents would consider using your service or product, you would definitely want to reconsider the validity of your concept or figure ways to promote it on a broader scale.

On the other hand, if your marketing research pointed out that 90 percent of the population thought it was a great idea and that 50 percent would have an immediate need for it, the potential for your business would be much greater, and proceeding with the idea would probably guarantee a profitable venture.

Buy an inexpensive notebook to help you keep track of your marketing data. Use a separate page for each category you are researching. The notebook will serve as your personal, ongoing market study to be reviewed and amended as your business grows and the audience you are serving changes.

Plan to update your information as new studies are published (generally an annual event), indicating changes in population, economy, or buying and spending trends. Most newspapers publish synopses of local, state, and federal studies of this nature, so maintain your notebook as appropriate. You should also reserve several pages to record comments and suggestions from customers

once your business is established, which will help you personalize the service to the market and keep you a step ahead of the competition.

Spend as much time as needed to feel comfortable about your marketing project. The important point is that the results of your research are comprehensive enough to provide you with concrete information on who your potential customers are and how you can best reach them.

Review

I have completed my entrepreneurial profile to determine my strengths and weaknesses. _____

My friends and family have given me additional input based on the profile. _____

I am aware of the advantages and disadvantages of going into business for myself. _____

Time is not a problem; I can easily devote the time I'll need to build my business. _____

The important people in my life are supportive of my decision. _____

I have analyzed my cash flow to ensure that I can support myself and my family for at least six months or until the business is solvent. _____

I feel confident about my future as a business owner at this point. _____

I know what people want as far as my business is concerned. _____

I have conducted informal studies to determine my potential customers and understand their needs. _____

I have analyzed the competition, know what they offer, and have a general idea about their success ratio. _____

I have done my marketing research and know how to get in touch with the audience I want to reach. _____

I have contacted the trade association for my industry and have accumulated facts and figures regarding the pros and cons of starting my own business. _____

I feel confident that my product or service is a marketable one. _____

Notes

Target Audience

Publications to Reach Audience

Additional Research Information

9

LOCATION: COMMERCIAL
VERSUS HOME-BASED

Where to Set Up the Business

Unless you have a substantial amount of start-up capital available to lease and equip a facility, you probably plan to start your catering business in your home, as many successful owners have done. While many caterers do all their cooking in their home kitchen and transport the finished product to the site of the event, there are others who prefer to use the client's kitchen for food preparation whenever possible.

There are several advantages to the latter option. One is the savings in utility costs. The second is that the prepared food can be served fresh and hot. The third advantage is that this option allows you to bypass health department and zoning commission regulations, which may prevent you from operating a food-service business from your home.

You might also consider exploring the options listed below as a way to start. Later, when your business grows, you can establish your kitchen in a commercial location.

1. Restrict your business to *only* those jobs that permit you to do the majority of cooking at the location where the function will be held. You can use your own kitchen for much of the preparation, such as slicing vegetables, making salads and desserts, and marinating meat. Many caterers purposely limit their business to on-site catering. This is one way of getting your business off the ground with low overhead and minimal start-up capital.

2. Scout your area for clubs or organizations that may have seldom-used kitchens on the premises. Many golf clubs, yacht clubs, groups like the Elks or Masons, and community centers have fully-equipped facilities that they use for their functions. It may be possible to rent the kitchen, or even to trade your catering services for kitchen usage.

 Also investigate churches, synagogues, and schools. One of the major advantages of this option is that the facility has undoubtedly been licensed and approved for on-site cooking by local authorities such as the Board of Health and the fire department.

3. Consider arranging a cooperative partnership with a restaurant that serves only breakfast and lunch. You may be able to rent or sublease the premises after hours for your own cooking. Again, restaurants will have the necessary licenses and cooking equipment.

Commercial Locations

If you have between $30,000 and $75,000 start-up capital and the desire to open your catering company in a commercial location, look for a space that has a kitchen of at least 1,000 square feet. Regardless of your budget, the location should have the potential to be converted to a full-size service kitchen with segregated areas for food preparation, storage space, and equipment and supplies. You will also need an office space to plan menus, organize assignments, handle record keeping, and talk to clients and employees in person or on the telephone. In most areas, you can save money on the rent by locating in an industrial or manufacturing area.

Although you will not be preparing food that is going to be consumed on the premises, it is necessary to obtain the required licenses. The Board of Health and your city or county clerk's office can tell you over the telephone if the area and the building are zoned for a catering business. The Board of Health and the fire department will inspect the premises before issuing their approval.

There are some defeats more triumphant than victories.

de Montaigne

The commercial space should be large enough to accommodate all initial and future equipment purchases, including stove, oven, microwave, refrigerator, freezer, mixer, slicer, oversized blender, large pots and pans, and worktables.

An Efficient Work Space

In planning your layout, think about traffic patterns between refrigerator and sink, sink and worktable, worktable and loading areas, etc. The more people working in the kitchen, the more you will appreciate a carefully planned design. Employees will be able to work under efficient, pleasant conditions.

To increase productivity in the kitchen, paint the walls a light color and provide good ventilation and lighting. A little background music will help to keep motivation high during tedious jobs.

The Home Kitchen

Catering enterprises, at least in the start-up stage, are ideal as home businesses. However, whether you'll be permitted to operate such a business from your home will depend on local zoning ordinances, perhaps your landlord, or other restrictions. Laws pertaining to the operation of your catering business vary by county and state. It's illegal to conduct a home-based business in certain counties, while in many others across the country it is acceptable as long as local requirements are met.

A fair amount of space is required for a catering business, whether at home or in a commercial location. Catering requires a

fully loaded kitchen, ample storage and counter space, and a desk area.

By operating your catering business from your home, you can save much-needed capital that would otherwise be spent on a commercial location. That money could go toward your all-important early-stage marketing.

Unlike businesses that lend themselves to use of a spare room or attic, catering requires the use of one of the busiest rooms in the home. If you choose to start your catering business at home, be sensitive to the needs of your family or roommates. As for the office area, it is best to have a permanent base of operations where you can leave unfinished work without its being disturbed and where you have a place to put supplies and business records for easy access. If at all avoidable, do not attempt to do bookkeeping and other functions at the kitchen table or on a folding card table. You will find yourself spending countless hours having to put things away or move them somewhere else to accommodate family life.

One or two good-sized bookcases should be more than enough space for storage and reference materials. You will want to keep on hand several cookbooks, recipe files, and culinary magazines.

Setting Up Your Business at Home

There is a lot of appeal in operating your business from home. Thousands of successful businesses have been started in a basement, a spare room, or on the kitchen table. It's true that Henry Ford founded the Ford Motor Company in his garage and Jean Nidetch started Weight Watchers in her living room as a support group for friends who wanted to lose weight. Both of these businesses, and many more like them, became successful multimillion-dollar corporations despite humble beginnings.

Starting a home-based business has provided an opportunity for many people who might otherwise never have the chance to become business owners. Women, especially, have discovered that they can build a profitable, satisfying business at home while still being available for their families.

For others, a home-based business is the ticket out of the world of the urban commuter. In fact, a home-based business is

the perfect way to try something new to see how it works while still working another job to pay the bills. Once the business has proven itself and is realizing a profit, you can leave the job to devote all your time to your new venture.

Couples often find that investing time and energy in building a business together at home develops stronger relationships in addition to increasing joint income. For the retired and for those with minor physical disabilities, it is a path to staying involved, exploring self-sufficiency, and guaranteeing that there can be a profitable future.

Start-ups Never Change

As with any new business, whether located at home or in a commercial location, it is important to follow the basic guidelines for start-up, including conducting a market survey, drawing up a business plan, setting goals, reviewing capital needs and projected income, developing an advertising campaign, and establishing a professional image.

Advantages of a Home-Based Business

♦ Ability to start your business immediately

♦ Minimal start-up capital needed

♦ No rent or excessive setup charges for utilities

♦ Comfortable working conditions

♦ Reduced wardrobe expenses

♦ No commuting

♦ Tax benefits

♦ Elimination of office politics

♦ Flexibility and independence

♦ Full utilization and recognition of skills

♦ Low risk for trial and error

A home-based catering business offers a number of advantages for the business owner who is just starting out. Setting up your business at home automatically eliminates up to 75 percent of the start-up costs and responsibilities required for a storefront operation. You are, in your home, already making rent or mortgage payments and paying for your own telephone service, insurance, and utilities. (In many instances, a commercial location will require $10,000 just to open the doors with basic leasehold improvements and/or equipment.) What's more, your home undoubtedly has a kitchen, meaning that until the time comes to upgrade, your equipment expenses are relatively minor. In addition, valuable time and energy are saved because you don't have to scout for the location, have utilities installed, and decorate the premises.

Getting Your Feet Wet

A home-based business gives you the opportunity to test the waters with a minimum of risk. This is especially beneficial to first-time entrepreneurs, who may prefer to learn and grow with the business in the comfort of home without the pressures that operating out of a commercial location often bring.

As a hedge against inflation, the home-based business is a natural. In addition to low start-up, tax deductions for use of a home office and business expenses provide relief from a seemingly endless outflow of cash spent on mortgage or rent payments. You must, however, be aware of the tax laws, which allow deductions only for that part of the home "used exclusively and regularly" for business and limited to a modified net income of the business.

After the business is running smoothly, you will find that the potential to earn money is greater because of reduced overhead. Your production will increase because you have more control over your schedule and fewer of the typical interruptions that arise in a commercial setting. Of course, as with any business arrangement, there are also disadvantages to setting up your business in your home. By recognizing them, however, it is possible to address and minimize the problems before they come up.

Getting Down to Work

One of the biggest problems faced by home-based entrepreneurs is being able to establish a productive work schedule. There are different types of interruptions that come up in a home environment, including visits from friends and neighbors, household chores that need to be done, the temptations of television shows or the daily newspaper when there is work to be produced, and the fact that there is no one around to spur you on.

A helpful suggestion for getting down to work is to dress in the morning as if you were going out to a regular job. This alone will help you set your priorities for the day.

The best solution, however, is to establish regular working hours at the outset (although you do have the flexibility as a home-based business owner to arrange your schedule around the times you know you are the most productive). If friends want to visit, politely explain to them that you are operating a business that requires your full concentration and arrange a suitable time to get together according to your schedule.

It is also important, if you have family, that they are supportive and willing to arrange their lives as much as possible around your schedule. This can be dealt with through frequent family discussions about what you are doing and how the business operates.

Disadvantages of a Home-Based Business

♦ Success is based 100 percent on your efforts

♦ Difficult to establish solid work habits

♦ Difficult to determine competitive rates

♦ Limited support system

♦ Isolation

♦ Limited work space

♦ Disruption of personal life

♦ Clients are uncomfortable coming to your home

♦ Zoning restrictions

Another difficult area is learning to separate business and pleasure. A home-based business often makes it very easy to work day and night on a project. Again, it is important to allot time for personal activities. The point to remember is that the work will get done much more efficiently if you are relaxed and rested.

It is also a good idea to have the business set up in a separate room or area that can be shut off from your personal living space after working hours. This will more easily enable you to separate work from leisure time.

Home-based business owners often experience feelings of isolation from those in their industry. One way to eliminate this is to join local groups, such as the chamber of commerce and networking groups, and to attend the meetings. Check to see how many members are entrepreneurs, which will give you a built-in support system. By making yourself available to serve on committees, you'll be able to reach into the community and publicize your business for the cost of your involvement.

Reviewing Local Laws

Before getting started, it is important to check that zoning ordinances in your area will allow you to use your home for business purposes. Since zoning ordinances vary from city to city and county to county, it is necessary to contact the planning department of your regional government offices or talk with your attorney to find out what is allowed, based on the type of business, the area to be used within your home, noise control, tax regulations, business signs, and other aspects, as well as if you need a special permit or license to operate.

If you are expecting clients to visit your home for business, it is best to have a separate room set up as an office so that when they do come to discuss your product or service, they won't feel as if they are intruding on a family. If, however, an office is out of the question, make sure you try to arrange meetings during times when the family is away from home to ensure that there will be no interruptions.

Another option is to go to the client's location for meetings. Depending on the business, however, and the quality of your work, client discomfort shouldn't be a major problem, according to a number of home-based business owners we have interviewed.

> *God gives every bird its food, but He does not throw it in the nest.*
>
> *J.G. Holland*

The bottom line, as far as the client is concerned, is—and will always be—reliable service and high-quality work provided in a professional atmosphere by a professional person.

The benefits of a home-based business to the beginning entrepreneur can mean the difference between working for someone else or turning a dream into reality. The key elements, as with any business, are motivation, a needed product or service, careful planning, and the desire to succeed. Just knowing that the expenses of establishing a business in a commercial location are alleviated by setting up a home-based enterprise is enough to push you forward to success, one small step after another.

Utilities and Phone

The home-based business has an additional advantage: Your phone line and utilities are already in place. Any additional equipment is easy to obtain from your utility carriers because you already have an established payment history.

Single-line telephone systems are adequate for most small businesses, but when your business outgrows a single-line system, you'll need a multiline system enabling you to accept several calls simultaneously and switch between lines.

Regardless of whether you need a single-line or a multiline system, some options are now available when choosing phone equipment.

Programmable memory allows automatic storage and instant dialing of phone numbers by pressing a button or entering a code.

Automatic redial reconnects the last number dialed, in some cases redialing at specific intervals until the call goes through.

Speed dialing allows you to quickly access frequently dialed numbers by using a one- to four-digit code.

Call waiting is especially useful for businesses with single lines, allowing you to take incoming calls while putting the original caller on hold.

Conference calling is often a related feature of call waiting, allowing you to simultaneously speak with two or more parties at different locations.

Call forwarding routes incoming calls to a preprogrammed phone number at another location.

Cordless phones are especially useful for the home business, allowing you to make or accept calls from any location in the house. Because cordless phones vary in quality, it's strongly recommended that you research the market thoroughly before buying.

Speaker phones allow you to carry on conversations without the constraint of holding a receiver. One of the main benefits is that you can accomplish other tasks while waiting on hold. They're also useful for note taking and similar chores during business conversations.

Voice mail is a combination answering, routing, and messaging system that can help cut front-office payroll costs (if you have a staff) while maximizing efficiency. Customers dialing a

voice-mail number are greeted by a recorded message and given a menu of options: direct-dialing employees in other departments, leaving messages for one or more individuals, receiving additional recorded information, and using the voice-mail system with a rotary-dial phone.

The cost of voice mail has been scaled down dramatically in recent years and is now available for small or even one-person businesses, presenting a first-class image while actually saving you money (not only in payroll costs but in avoiding potential lost revenues from unanswered or misdirected calls).

Long-Distance Carriers

Whether you're a one-person, home-based operation or an expanding business in a commercial location, long-distance service is, of course, essential.

The host of carriers competing for your long-distance dollar, their conflicting claims, and a wide range of services can bewilder the small business owner trying to make a choice.

When deciding which carrier to use for your business, consider the following:

◆ Areas of the country and the world that you will most frequently be calling

◆ Monthly amount you anticipate spending on long-distance calls

◆ Time of day you'll be making most of your calls

◆ Seasonal calling patterns

◆ Whether you'll be dealing only with clients statewide (a regional WATS line would be a cost-effective choice)

In addition, read the various carriers' promotional information carefully. Does the carrier you're considering charge start-up or installation fees or a flat monthly fee? If the latter, will you meet the carrier's minimum usage requirements and are the services offered worth the monthly charge?

Other factors to consider include available volume discounts based on usage and dedicated lines giving you exclusive access to a telecommunications network.

800 Numbers

Businesses that market products and services regionally or nationally have found the 800 number to be one of their most effective marketing tools. Customers who might not otherwise pay for a long-distance call now pick up the phone without hesitation—and frequently wind up requesting further information about services or making hefty credit card purchases.

Though 800 numbers can pay for themselves thousands of times over, the installation fees, service charges, and usage fees can be expensive. Consider carefully whether the potential costs outweigh the benefits. An alternative is the localized 800 number, available for small, highly targeted geographic areas. Consult your phone company's service representative for further information.

Guidelines for Commercial Locations

Once volume expands to a certain point, you may need to move to a commercial location. Selecting the right location is vital to the success of your business. The first two factors you must analyze when looking for a commercial location are

1. The community you want to live and/or work in, based on family needs, finances, your preference for a particular area because of health reasons, or the fact that you have an established reputation in a certain area
2. The locations available within that community

These factors are interrelated. You may want to settle down in an area with a limited number of suitable business locations available. Or you may have run across a number of viable sites in several communities or locations, in which case an investigation of each must be conducted, covering each of the following points:

1. *The type of business you are planning to operate.*
 Remember that retail, wholesale, and service businesses
 have slightly different requirements as determined by the
 type of product or service being offered and the market
 potential in a specific area.

2. *The demographics of the area.* You should find out the
 number of consumers who want or need your product or
 service and are willing and able to pay your price, the
 median income and employment opportunities, the age
 ranges of the major population group, and the volume of
 retail trade and projected expansion data (available from
 census reports and chamber of commerce business re-
 ports accumulated during your market research project).

3. *Competition.* You must determine how many other simi-
 lar establishments are serving the market and how their
 businesses are going to decide if there is room for your
 new venture. The best way to do this is by making a list
 of businesses from the phone book that you feel will be
 in direct competition and, if feasible, visiting their loca-
 tions at different times of day. Observe the activity levels
 and talk with employees, who should be willing to answer
 your questions if you approach them in a friendly way.
 Often, the same kind of research can be accomplished on
 the telephone.

4. *Traffic patterns.* Is your proposed location close to
 freeways, major intersections, and/or a central business
 district? Is there sufficient parking? Is the foot traffic past
 the location strong and steady enough to guarantee
 walk-in trade that will generate sales and profits? The
 ease with which customers can get to your location is a
 major consideration in terms of success.

5. *Your image.* Before you go scouting for locations, decide
 on the image you want to project, such as quality products
 at good prices, superior service, and convenience.

6. *The product or service.* If, for example, you were
 planning to sell high-priced, state-of-the-art European
 electronic equipment, it would be advisable to locate your

business in a mall or on the main street of an economically comfortable community to ensure getting the response you need to survive. Generally, there are specific areas within a marketplace that cater to consumers in specific income brackets and/or occupational groups, i.e., executives, blue-collar workers, students, etc. Consider your product/service and the projected number of potential buyers within the community.

7. *The amount of rent required.* Locations having the highest potential of profit through consumer traffic (such as a prime downtown site or shopping mall, a corner shop, or a store with good frontage) are more expensive because competition keeps rents up to the maximum. The trade-off is an increase in sales and a lower advertising budget because of the visibility factor.

Retail Businesses

The guidelines indicated above are applicable for retail businesses. Poor location is one of the chief causes of failure among retail stores, but, on the other hand, the right location can be all it takes for even a mediocre business to thrive and grow.

Service Businesses

When clients are going to be visiting your place of business, the same principles of location selection apply as are indicated for retail. If clients will not be visiting, location selection can be based on rent, the amount of space needed, and the convenience to you.

Wholesale, Manufacturing, or Mail-Order Businesses

Where you locate a wholesale business depends on your market. If dealing primarily with local retailers or customers, your location should be within easy driving distance of your clientele.

However, if most of your business is conducted through the mail or delivery services, you can base your selection on the best rent available and the convenience factor for you and your staff. When choosing a location for your wholesale business, warehousing needs are a vital consideration, as is projected expansion.

Before Signing a Lease

Unless you're planning to purchase the commercial location, rent your location from a family member or accept a temporary agreement in a location that is for sale. But keep in mind that you will be required to sign a lease before moving in. The most desirable agreement for you as a new business owner is a one- to two-year lease with a renewal option and a guaranteed rate for rent increases over a five- to ten-year period.

Rent for a commercial location is established either on a flat rate or a percentage basis. Under the flat rate, rent is generally based on the square footage of the shop and on the location or, in some cases, on potential volume. The percentage base involves a base amount of rent plus a prearranged percentage of monthly sales.

Your lease will also cover a number of other points, such as the liabilities and responsibilities of the landlord and of you, the tenant; i.e., who is to pay for utilities, specific repairs, renovations, tax increases, etc.

The lease may contain stipulations about the size of the exterior sign you can erect, hours of operation, insurance coverage, and assignation of the lease to another party (a sublet).

Before signing a lease to set up your business, make sure that electrical lines are adequate enough to handle high-volume usage, that you have restrooms for employees and/or clients, and that there are convenient parking areas. Also check with the leasing agent to be certain you can make leasehold improvements, e.g., storage shelves, at your discretion as the business warrants it.

It is recommended that you have an attorney review the lease carefully before you sign it to ensure you understand all of the clauses and to serve as a negotiator, if necessary.

Review

If setting up my business at home, I have

Checked with the city and county offices in my area regarding required licenses and permits and zoning regulations for the home office _____

Set aside a room or an area in my home that will be used exclusively for my business _____

Installed a separate telephone line and purchased an answering machine, or contracted with an answering service _____

Set up a separate business bank account _____

Informed friends and family of my business routine and specific working hours to reduce interruptions and distractions _____

If setting up in a commercial location, I have

Investigated rental rates for the area I am interested in leasing _____

Checked traffic flow, parking, and foot traffic around my proposed location _____

Determined that my business is compatible with others in the area _____

Talked with my prospective landlord about improvements, maintenance, and rent increases _____

Had my lawyer check the rental agreement and any local zoning regulations _____

Secured the necessary operating licenses and permits from the city and/or county _____

Notes

Key Points

Possible Locations

Size and Floor Plan Considerations

10

PROFESSIONAL BACKUP

From the start-up stage and as your business continues to grow and prosper, you will need the assistance of several professionals, including a lawyer, an accountant, and an insurance agent.

The best way to find a professional is, according to the majority of business owners, through personal recommendations from other entrepreneurs, especially those in similar businesses as yours, and from friends or relatives. The most important factor is that the person doing the recommending understand exactly what you will need from the professional you will be hiring.

For example, your cousin's divorce lawyer is probably not as well suited to helping you draw up a partnership agreement as the attorney a friend used for help with incorporating his business.

Before making a decision, talk to several recommended professionals until you find someone who can best satisfy your needs for the business as outlined below and who has a fee structure you can afford.

Equally important: Your choice should be someone you feel comfortable with, especially during periods when you find yourself having to call several times a week to resolve a problem or complete a specific task.

In many cases, because attorneys and accountants often work on a particular business matter in conjunction with one another, the attorney you select may be able to suggest an accountant who can properly service your business, or vice versa.

If you're planning to hire an attorney or an accountant, you should start interviewing likely candidates eight to nine months prior to the date you plan to start the business. This will give you time to find a suitable match and give the attorney time to take care of all pre-start-up functions, such as assisting in the structure of your business or helping with your business plan.

Professional Services

Legal

An attorney with broad-based expertise in business can help you with such matters as raising capital; the legal and tax ramifications and benefits of various business forms including sole proprietorship, partnership, or corporation; name clearance to ensure that you are not using a name already designated by another company; legal tips on operating in your desired location; and help you file all necessary legal papers and documents needed for financing, establishing your business form, and so on.

He or she will review contracts and lease agreements and can provide support with collection problems. The lawyer you select should also be willing and able to represent you in the event of any claims that are brought against you or lawsuits you initiate.

Fees

Depending on your attorney's expertise, reputation, and the market he or she serves (metropolitan area versus small town, for example), fees will differ dramatically.

In a small community, lawyers often charge a set rate for the job being done, while "city" lawyers typically charge by the hour.

This does not include the extraneous expenses involved, such as the cost of incorporating, which depends on the state you operate in. Neither do these fees include supplemental costs, such

as travel and telephone, incurred by the attorney in the handling of your case.

A good way to determine the range of fees in your area is to check with your local chamber of commerce or the state bar association, generally located in the capital city. The bar association may also be able to provide you with information about a particular attorney's reputation and expertise.

When talking with potential attorneys—and when you have found one who is compatible with your needs—always be sure to ask for an outline of expenses and if he or she is willing to notify you when the fees for a particular task will be exceeded.

Accounting

The accountant you select should, early on, be able to work with you on assembling your business plan, including your projected profit and loss statements, for financing.

Down the line, as your business is being established, the accountant will help you set up your books and, once in operation, should handle your tax returns, prepare financial statements, and offer financial advice regarding tax matters, cash flow, investments to maximize the use of profits, and the tax regulations regarding employees when you are ready to hire.

Fees

As with attorneys, there is a professional association in your state capital that certifies and maintains records on the reputation and fee structures of accountants.

The basis for fee structuring does vary slightly, however, with accountants. Some charge by the hour, others by the day, and still others work on a set monthly retainer based on the estimated amount of time they will be required to spend on your work.

Insurance

Before setting out on your search for an insurance agent, it is advisable to have already established your business form and learned exactly what insurance the law in your area requires you

to carry (fire, liability, etc.) and, if hiring employees, what kind of program you'll be offering employees, as well as your own needs for medical and life insurance.

The insurance agent you choose should be familiar with the needs of businesses and business owners, not just the standard life and disability policies. Your insurance needs will change as your business grows and expands (i.e., employee health, workers' compensation, etc.). At that point, you may want to consider key-person coverage to ensure that your company can survive if a major partner or employee dies.

There are also a number of pension programs and stock-option programs available in the event you want to offer employees the incentive to increase their participation in the company in exchange for partial "ownership" down the line.

Fees

The fees for your agent's expertise are paid from your premiums, and there should be no extra charge for advice or administration of your insurance policies and programs.

Professional Services

Legal

Accounting

Insurance

11

TAXES, LICENSES, AND PERMITS

As a business owner, you are responsible for timely filing and payment of federal, state, and local taxes. Whether you have an accountant prepare your returns or you do it yourself, the task will be made much easier if you establish a systematic record-keeping system (as described in Chapter 15) and keep your records accurate and up-to-date.

This includes maintaining all written documents pertaining to the financial aspect of your business: invoices, bank statements, receipts of any and all business expenses, and deposit slips.

One of the easiest ways to keep control of the "paper dragon" is to set up a 9 x 12-inch manila envelope or a file folder for each of the following categories:

♦ *Paid Bills*—both personal and business

♦ *Sales Receipts* of every product you've sold or service job you've performed

♦ *Inventory* records based on ongoing inventory control and quarterly audits

♦ *Copies of Invoices* or billing statements that are paid, with a separate file for those still due you

♦ **_Receipts_** for miscellaneous cash purchases

♦ **_Auto/Entertainment_** receipts from travel and promotional activities

All of these documents must be kept for at least five years to substantiate deductions claimed on your income tax returns in the event of an Internal Revenue Service (IRS) audit. Make up new file folders or envelopes at the beginning of each year and store the old ones in a safe place.

Preparing income tax returns is not only a time-consuming task that can take you away from the important job of running your business, but also somewhat of an art form. Tax law is a constantly changing, complicated fact of life. It is strongly recommended that you have an accountant lined up to prepare your taxes and to keep you informed of any pertinent changes during the year.

Business Deductions

The deductions that you will most likely qualify for as a business owner include operating expenses such as telephone, postage, advertising, bank service charges, travel and expense of conventions, interest, dues to professional organizations, and subscriptions to magazines pertaining to your business, among others.

> *Operating your business from home allows you to deduct not only a substantial portion of your rent or mortgage payment, but also percentages of your phone and utility expenses.*

If you have established your business at home, you will be able to deduct that portion of the house used exclusively for business, as well as a percentage of your costs for telephone service and utilities.

Again, because of the complexity and obscurity of many of the deductions, it is best to have a professional prepare your taxes to ensure you get the full benefits to which you are entitled. Filing requirements will be determined by the type of business, the legal structure (sole proprietorship, partnership, or corporation), income from the business, your

location, state and local laws, and whether or not you have employees.

For example, as the sole proprietor of your business you would probably only be required to file personal federal and state returns based on profit or loss, with the appropriate schedules for business expenses, pay scales, self-employment and estimated taxes, and local business license fees and sales taxes.

State Income Tax

Each state has corresponding filing requirements; however, form and schedule numbers vary. Contact your state franchise tax board or your accountant for details.

Local Taxes

Taxes will vary from city to city and county to county; however, you *may* be required to pay city income tax and local sales tax as well as real or personal property taxes. Check with your local government offices for specifics.

Licenses and Permits

To operate your business, you will need permits and licenses based on the requirements in your area and the type of business you are operating. You will probably be required to obtain the following documents regardless of where you live.

Local Business License

Basically, this is simply a fee paid to the city or county where you are located that allows you to operate your business in that area. Some cities will also require you to pay a percentage of your gross sales every year.

Fictitious Name Statement

This is a registration for protection of your business name. Filing the fictitious name statement will also involve a city- or county-wide search to make sure you are not duplicating an existing name. This can be done at your county hall of records.

Seller's Permit or Resale Certificate

This is required only if you are going to be charging sales tax. Services are often exempt.

Health Permit

This is required only if you are preparing or distributing food in any manner, and involves an initial inspection and periodic follow-up inspections by health department officials.

Taxpayer Identification Number

This is available from the IRS in the case of partnerships, Subchapter S corporations, or corporations. Sole proprietors are required to have a taxpayer identification number if they pay wages to one or more employees or file pension or excise tax forms.

Your local governmental offices or your attorney will be able to give you specific licenses and permits required, as well as the corresponding fees for each as they apply to your business.

Legal Structure

As a self-employed business owner, you are required to decide on a legal form of business for tax reporting purposes. There are four basic classifications, as outlined below. If, after reviewing them, you are still unsure of which way to go, it would be advisable to talk with a lawyer about the advantages and disadvantages of each structure for your particular business.

All businesses, regardless of size, are required to maintain detailed records and file the necessary tax returns. In a corporation, regular meetings must be held. The stockholders elect a board of directors, who establish and monitor corporate policy. The board selects corporate officers to conduct the day-to-day operations of the business.

Sole proprietorships are the most convenient and least complicated form of organization for new business owners, especially in the early stages. As your business grows, you will want to explore the options as a way of protecting your personal assets and increasing the potential for expansion capital.

Sole Proprietorship

This is the easiest to establish and is the structure many small business owners choose. A proprietorship is relatively free from government regulation, as the business has no existence apart from the owner. Profits from the operation of the business are treated as personal income for purposes of taxation, and your proprietary interest ends when you die or dissolve the business.

The major drawback of a proprietorship is that you are personally liable for any and all claims against the business and undertake the risks of the business to the extent of all assets, whether they are used in the business or personally owned. As a sole proprietor, you will be required to file self-employment tax returns and ordinarily would have to make estimated tax payments on a quarterly basis.

General Partnership

This is also an easy structure to set up and administer. Since responsibilities and capitalization are usually shared by two or more partners, taxation is based on each partner's share of business income and determined by their individual tax rates. Again, claims against the business can be filed against personal assets, and financial liability is shared equally by all partners.

Limited Partnership

This structure can be established when one or more people are willing to invest cash or tangible property in the business with active participation in the daily operations. However, there must be at least one general partner who carries unlimited financial liability and who usually maintains a full-time managerial position within the company.

The limited partners are only liable for business debts up to the amount of their investment. Although a partnership is not a taxable entity, it must figure its profit or loss and file an annual tax return, which also becomes part of the partners' personal returns.

Corporation

In this structure, stock or shares in the business are sold to investors or stockholders, who then control the company. The advantage is that corporate stockholders are removed from any liability against personal assets. The most anyone can lose in the event of bankruptcy or a liability claim is his or her stock.

The privilege of reduced liability, however, creates paperwork (articles of incorporation and annual reports for the state tax commission and federal regulators), expenses (filing and licensing fees), and double taxation (the corporation is taxed on profits, while stockholders and elected officers are taxed individually on wages and/or dividend income).

Subchapter S Corporations

This structure has proved to be a real boon for small business owners who want the benefit of corporate protection from personal liability without double taxation. In a Subchapter S corporation, a maximum of thirty-five stockholders (who can be family members) report their share of corporate income on individual tax returns.

The corporation itself is generally exempt from federal income tax; however, it may be required to pay a tax on excess net passive investment income, capital gains, or built-in gains. To structure your company as a Subchapter S corporation, all of the shareholders must consent to the choice.

Notes

Key Points

Personal Thoughts

Additional Research

12

NAMING YOUR BUSINESS

$\mathbf{A}$s a pet owner, it is unlikely that you would give your German shepherd a name like Fifi. It wouldn't suit the dog's image, nor would it be appropriate. The same principle applies to choosing a name for your business.

The name you select for your business can be a tremendous asset when it defines the kind of image you want to project. You want the name to attract and appeal to potential customers, to be easily remembered over that of the competition's, and be appropriate to the type of business you are starting.

Today's consumers are constantly bombarded with advertising as they go about their daily routines. Getting their attention, and holding it long enough for them to make an association between your business name and what you are offering, is imperative.

A memorable moniker can mean the difference between continued growth or a mediocre response from an audience victimized by information overload. (It is, of course, important to keep in mind that your ultimate success depends on well-designed advertising, careful planning, and quality products and/or service.)

Naming Your Catering Business

Take some time to think about this, because your company name needs to fulfill several functions beyond identifying you. The name you choose can affect a customer's perceptions of your legitimacy.

It may serve you best to just use your own name, e.g., Katie Smith Catering Services. If you want to point out a specialty, such as gourmet food or business catering, you can work that emphasis into the name you choose.

Depending on where you live, there may be a number of other catering services with names that are similar to the one you want. Look through the Yellow Pages to research the names of other catering businesses, and then set yourself apart from the flock. Choose a name that is catchy and descriptive, and then come up with a logo that says something about who you are.

Brainstorming

Start by making a list of all the positive aspects of your business that you can think of, and call on friends and relatives to provide as many as they can come up with. Write down all the possibilities, no matter how funny or unusual they seem. A handy tool for business naming is the thesaurus, which will give you a vast number of options for commonplace names. Consider everything that springs forth from your imagination.

When you have created a list of likely candidates, get together with a group of supportive friends and family members and have a brainstorming session to either pick one of the choices you have come up with or to develop something from the ideas listed. Chances are that within a few hours, you will have a name for your business.

Catchy names are fun to design. However, make sure it isn't so offbeat, cute, or trendy as to risk slipping into obscurity as time passes.

The Fictitious Name Statement

You are required to file a fictitious name statement with the county clerk's office where you will be basing the business. While there,

you should be able to do a countywide name check on the spot to see if there are any other businesses in the region using the name you have selected. The filing fee depends on where you live, and must be done within thirty days after you officially open your business.

It will also be necessary to publish the fictitious name in a local newspaper; the cost depends on the circulation of the paper. The county clerk's office will advise you about specific requirements in your area.

If you are starting a business that will be operating in a broader market, statewide or nationally, it is important to have your attorney do a name clearance investigation, which can take from three days to three weeks.

Your Visual Image

After you have selected a name that reflects your business image, the next step is translating it into a visual symbol or logo (logotype) to serve as the signature piece for your business. Often this involves creating a visual interpretation of your company name, but in other cases a graphic symbol or trademark is designed to serve as identification.

Some established corporate trademarks are so familiar that you can immediately identify the company even without seeing or hearing its name.

A good example of this includes the logo of the dog with his head cocked to one side. The accompanying copy reads "His Master's Voice," and it's a good bet that you recognize this as the logo for RCA. Another effective logo is the avant-garde apple that identifies Apple computer products.

If you do not have the graphic skills necessary to design a logo with impact, get in touch with your nearest art association (listed in the phone book or available through local art supply shops or galleries) or call a nearby college or university. Ask the head of the art department if your design can be given as a class assignment or if he or she could recommend a student to do the job for a small fee. It will give students practical application, and the design can be used later in their portfolios. You can offer cash or a prize for the best design. The students will undoubtedly meet

the challenge with enthusiasm and give you a number of good samples and ideas from which to choose.

Selecting a Typeface

Save sample logos and advertisements that use a typeface you like. Type is an extremely important element of logo design and can also pinpoint the precise image you hope to express. Type not only presents the basic message, it can play a powerful role in the overall appearance of your logo and can actually create atmosphere. A chart of some of the more popular typefaces is included at the end of this chapter.

When deciding on a typeface for your logo, visit print shops or typesetting studios and look at their typeface books. They offer both the usual, functional varieties as well as a selection of unique typefaces that can really dress up your logo and subtly portray a specific personality such as dignified, fun, powerful, classic, or cutting edge.

Historically, in developing business names, simplicity has scored the highest points. The name you choose should be short, to the point, and easy for consumers to pronounce.

Have the logo and your business information (address, phone number, etc.) set in more than the one typeface so that you can see how they will look when printed. Also ask to have them set in both small (10- to 12-point for business cards) and larger (20- to 24-point for letterhead) versions. Once typeset, you will be able to make a final decision about which typeface suits the image you want to project.

Typesetters generally have a minimum fee based on the amount of time they spend on a job, which can vary from $15 per hour in a small city to $50 per hour in a business area, and as high as $100 per hour in major metropolitan areas. That's why it's important to shop around.

Word processing specialists or independent desktop publishers can also provide a variety of typefaces and formats at less

expense. Since you will only be having a few words typeset, the time and cost required to set them in several different styles should certainly be affordable.

Business Cards and Stationery

The typeface and logo you eventually choose will be used on your letterhead; in your display and telephone advertising; on all promotional materials, including flyers, brochures, and announcements; on your sign; and on statements and invoices.

They will also be used on your business cards, one of the most inexpensive and convenient ways to inform people about your service or product. Once you have had cards printed, be generous. Give one to everyone you meet and always be sure to carry a supply wherever you go.

Most fast-print copy centers are prepared to help you if you decide not to design your own business cards and stationery. They have samples of business forms, letterheads, and cards with various styles to choose from. Make sure that your company name, logo, address, and phone number are included where necessary. If you have a fax and/or toll-free number, be sure those numbers are included. When someone looks at your card or letterhead, it must tell them instantly who you are, what your business is, and how you can be reached.

Sample Typefaces

Helvetica
ABCDEFGHIJ
abcdefghij

Britannic Light
ABCDEFGHIJ
abcdefghij

Garamond Book
ABCDEFGHIJ
abcdefghij

Helvetica Black
ABCDEFGHIJ
abcdefghij

Britannic Bold
ABCDEFGHIJ
abcdefghij

Garamond Ultra
ABCDEFGHIJ
abcdefghij

Helvetica Condensed
ABCDEFGHIJ
abcdefghij

Brush Script
ABCDEFGHIJ
abcdefghij

Times Roman
ABCDEFGHIJ
abcdefghij

ITC Eras
ABCDEFGHIJ
abcdefghij

Optima
ABCDEFGHIJ
abcdefghij

Times Italic
ABCDEFGHIJ
abcdefghij

ITC Eras Demi
ABCDEFGHIJ
abcdefghij

Optima Italic
ABCDEFGHIJ
abcdefghij

ITC Fenice Regular
ABCDEFGHIJ
abcdefghij

ITC Eras Bold
ABCDEFGHIJ
abcdefghij

Optima Bold
ABCDEFGHIJ
abcdefghij

ITC Fenice Bold
ABCDEFGHIJ
abcdefghij

Korinna
ABCDEFGHIJ
abcdefghij

Park Avenue
ABCDEFGHIJ
abcdefghij

ITC Fenice Ultra
ABCDEFGHIJ
abcdefghij

Korinna Bold
ABCDEFGHIJ
abcdefghij

Palatino
ABCDEFGHIJ
abcdefghij

Eurostile
ABCDEFGHIJ
abcdefghij

Rose Round
ABCDEFGHIJ
abcdefghij

Palatino Italic
ABCDEFGHIJ
abcdefghij

Eurostile Bold
ABCDEFGHIJ
abcdefghij

Lubalin Graph
ABCDEFGHIJ
abcdefghij

Palatino Bold
ABCDEFGHIJ
abcdefghij

Eurostile Extend
ABCDEFGHIJ
abcdefghij

Notes

Key Points

Personal Thoughts

Additional Research

13

DEVELOPING A BUSINESS PLAN

Developing your business plan is the most important process you will undertake in your career as an entrepreneur, regardless of the size or type of business you have decided to start.

A well-thought-out business plan will serve as a blueprint while your idea turns into a recognizable entity and as it grows into a stable and profitable venture. Too often we hear former small business owners say they probably could have made a success of their business if they had only known what to expect from the beginning...and that is where the business plan comes in.

Unfortunately, too many new entrepreneurs are unfamiliar with the importance of planning, or consider themselves an exception and feel they can succeed by winging it or dealing with problems as they arise. Not true!

Every business, whether a large commercial venture or a small home-based enterprise, needs to analyze its potential, examine its strengths and weaknesses, and determine the future of the organization. It works for the major corporations and it will work for you, especially once you become involved in the day-to-day operations of the business. Having a business plan will give you the freedom to follow the steps you have carefully laid out with

regard to budgeting, the success ratio of your product or service, the hiring of employees, and other growth decisions.

Advantages of the Business Plan

Once you have made the decision to become a business owner, you must devise a specific statement that clearly outlines *what* you plan to do, *when* you plan to do it, and *how* you will accomplish the short- and long-term goals.

Not only will this keep you on track, it will serve as an indicator to others of your sincerity and knowledge when you go out to find start-up or expansion capital, and it will serve as the foundation of your financing proposal.

The other advantage is that the actual task of putting your business plan together will help you define and clarify every step of your concept and, if done in a conscientious and objective manner, will point out potential trouble spots that can be addressed before they become major problems.

If all the necessary components are covered, it will put your business on the road to profit. It is a sure bet that, down the road, if you find your business is not generating the income you had originally projected, this is because you didn't include one or more of the basic business plan requirements.

Not a Guessing Game

Like any other major project, preparing a business plan involves time and research. It shouldn't be a guessing game. It will be necessary to ask yourself some very specific questions and to answer them thoughtfully and honestly. The business plan is your foundation, so build it carefully to ensure that it works at optimum efficiency for your needs. And make sure it is typed, orderly, and good looking so that you and others can recognize its importance in the professional scheme of your expanding operation.

An important aspect to remember is that your business plan is not cast in stone. In fact, what makes a business plan so great is that it invites revisions as your business changes and grows. This makes it a companion in your success and, by reviewing it regularly, a partner in your progress.

The best way to approach your business plan is to take paper and pen and devote a few hours to coming up with some hard answers. Of course, you will want to condense your answers to fit into specific segments within the plan, including (in order of appearance) Concept and Feasibility, Legal Structure, Product or Service, Customer Base, Marketing and Production Goals, Personnel (your résumé and Entrepreneurial Profile and those of any other key personnel), and Financial Statements.

It is advisable to start each segment on a separate page and to create a table of contents to place in the front. Be sure it is well-written and organized, neatly typed, and bound in a report folder to preserve it and give it a professional look, especially when using it as a sales tool to convince lenders.

Key Questions to Ask Yourself

The first question you must ask yourself is "Why am I interested in this particular business?" Probably the answer will be something to the effect of wanting to be your own boss and making money...independence and income.

This answer is fine as a personal goal, but it isn't going to be good enough if you are planning to approach potential lenders for funding. They will want to see an overview of your business concept, why you are convinced it will be successful, and where it fits in the scheme of similar businesses in your town or city.

The next question you must ask is "What is my product or service?" This may seem like a ridiculous question since you know what your product or service is, but it goes deeper. Your written response will include details about the service or a description of your product (preferably positive), with a focus on why customers will be inclined to work with you.

Additional questions to consider should include:

◆ Why do I believe there is a need for my product or service?

◆ How do I plan to develop my business over the next five years?

◆ How much will I charge to ensure value to the customer and profit for myself?

◆ Who are my suppliers?

◆ Who are my customers?

◆ What equipment do I need to start the business?

◆ How much inventory and supplies do I need for start-up?

◆ What will it cost?

◆ Who are my competitors and where are they located?

◆ What does the competition offer and how will I offer something different to attract customers?

◆ What changes are occurring in my marketing area that will impact my business in the future?

◆ What are my estimated sales figures for each of the next five years? (A guesstimate can be based on researching similar businesses in the area.)

◆ How will I advertise and promote my business and how will I pay for it?

◆ How and where is my product going to be manufactured?

◆ What is involved in the production—materials, labor, costs?

◆ Where will my service be performed?

◆ What equipment is required for my service and what are the costs for leasing versus purchasing?

◆ What are other overhead expenses (rent, employees, etc.)?

◆ How many people will be involved in the business and what are their qualifications?

◆ If I don't have employees, am I qualified to run the business myself?

By talking with people in similar businesses, suppliers and direct competitors, and your local chamber of commerce, you will gather a great deal of information, both positive and negative, about your potential business. People love to talk about their success and, if you ask in the right way, their failures.

If you operate like an investigative reporter for a few days while doing research for your business plan, it's guaranteed that

you will obtain plenty of good, solid information. A Service Corps of Retired Executives (SCORE) representative through the Small Business Administration can also provide assistance or tell you about resources that can help you develop a realistic business plan.

Trade associations, listed in reference books available at your local library, can provide you with invaluable details on industry facts and figures, such as the percentage of gross sales that should be spent on advertising, the percentage that is typically paid for rent in your particular business, and how to price your product or service.

The final item to include in this section of your business plan, when and if presenting it for financing, is a personal résumé, designed to emphasize your general business management experience and your expertise within your specific area.

Describe the job duties for every job you have held, including any special aspects that pertain directly to the business.

If you cannot prepare the résumé, it is worth the minor fee to have it done professionally. The results will pay for the cost hundreds of times over.

Financial Statements

Once you have written your overview and description sheets, it's time to get down to numbers. This is the key to your business plan and, unfortunately, the area where many entrepreneurs get bogged down. But without an understanding about the numbers involved, you can never expect to be a good manager and really shouldn't be surprised if you run into money problems within the first year.

Again, utilizing resources such as the chamber of commerce and trade associations, work up your financial pages to include the following components, which most lenders will want to see projected for one and five years.

> *Show me a person with an obsession about succeeding and a solid business plan, and I'll show you a good risk.*
>
> Anonymous
> Loan Officer

Projected operating expenses. This projected number includes materials, advertising, salaries for employees or outside labor, and other expenses directly related to the cost of doing business.

Estimate of gross (before tax) sales revenue. If the business is not yet operating, base your estimate on research figures from trade associations and what the local market dictates. If business is underway, base your estimate on how many items or hours of service you plan to sell and the average price you plan to charge.

How you arrived at the figures for these statements. Generally, you would base your figures on assumptions made about the number of months of operation, estimated number of sales, and the average amount versus the cost of each sale.

Cost of equipment and furnishings. Get estimated quotes, whether you are planning to purchase or lease these items.

Cost of materials. You need to know how much items will cost for production, if applicable, and for maintenance on equipment needed to run the business.

Additional operating expenses. You should research prices for rent, telephone and other utilities, business taxes and license fees, office supplies, and even decorating costs. Include a category called "Other" to provide a cushion for unexpected expenses.

Balance sheet. This shows assets, such as equipment and operating capital you already have, and liabilities or debts and expenses. If the business has not yet started, this would be a personal balance sheet indicating your net worth, listing all possessions of any value plus cash, stock, and other holdings, minus financial responsibilities.

Leasehold improvements. If you are planning to rent a commercial location or redesign a room at home strictly for business, estimate cleaning and restoration costs in this statement.

By investing the time and energy into this portion of the business plan, you will absorb the numbers into your consciousness and be able to recognize, at a glance, when your costs exceed your profit margin or when you are in a position to start expanding.

If money matters are absolutely beyond your comprehension at this point, it would pay to hire someone to work with you to

develop the financial pages of the plan. There are business consultants and accountants who will probably charge you a substantial amount, or you can approach the accounting or business department of the nearest college and see if there is a qualified student available to help you.

No matter who you find to assist you, however, be sure to stay involved in the process...the discipline and hard work will guarantee success.

Notes

Key Points

Personal Thoughts

Additional Research

14

FINANCING YOUR BUSINESS

Starting your business without having sufficient capital is setting yourself up for problems from the beginning. Undercapitalization is cited as one of the major reasons why businesses do not succeed; however, this simply boils down to bad planning.

If you research and record all the goals, marketing data, equipment and supply requirements, and financial needs of your venture before actually opening your doors, you will be able to see at a glance how much you need to get going, and *why you need it.* That way, there will be no surprises and no reason that your business should suffer from lack of capitalization.

It is important to have the financial resources to cover all your preliminary planning and start-up costs, including expenses incurred to research the feasibility of your business and expenses required to set up shop, from equipment and supplies to advertising and utility setup charges. In addition, you need a surplus to carry you over personally until the business becomes productive. The Cash Flow Statement and Start-up Costs Worksheet forms provided in Chapter 6, along with your Projected Expense Statement, will help you determine these expenses.

If, after developing your business plan (Chapter 13), you find that your personal resources are not enough to open the business, there are other options available.

The four most common methods include

- ◆ Starting the business on a part-time basis while holding a full-time job to cover expenses

- ◆ Taking on a limited partner

- ◆ Going to friends or family members for the money you need

- ◆ Applying for a loan through a commercial lender or the Small Business Administration (SBA)

There are, of course, pros and cons to each of these options.

Starting Out Part-time

Starting your business on a part-time or "moonlighting" basis is a decision that must be made based on the nature of the business. If you are planning to capitalize on your skills in upholstering, for example, you should have no trouble building up the business at night and on weekends.

It is perfectly feasible to start small, using your garage or a spare room as your production facility and purchasing an answering machine for potential customers to leave a message while you are at your regular job. When you get home, you simply call them back to discuss prices and arrange a time when it is convenient to pick up the piece of furniture to be upholstered.

On the other hand, if you are planning to start a temporary help agency, for example, it would be in your best interest to go into it on a full-time, dedicated basis, as your potential customers are going to want fast results and will call someone else if they are even slightly discouraged, such as getting a recorded message when they call.

Moonlighting will work with some businesses, but before exploring it as an option you must figure out if your limited availability will affect your credibility, if you really have the time and energy to work at a regular job and try to build a business (not to mention family responsibilities), and whether your ultimate

goal is to be self-employed or just to earn a few extra dollars to supplement your base income.

Considering a Partner

A limited partner is one who will put up the money you need and step into the background to let you run the business the way you see fit. You must be sure, however, to have your attorney draw up a precise partnership agreement that covers every eventuality. Partnerships are typically entered into with the best intentions and the unwavering belief that the business will be successful.

Since this is not always the case—and even if it were—it is a businesslike move to ensure that such aspects as decision making, distribution of profits and losses, contributions of partners, and handling disputes and changes are outlined and approved by all the partners.

Approaching a Lender

Once you have your business plan and other paperwork prepared, decide which lending association you want to approach. Certainly, if you have a stable record with a checking or savings account at your regular bank or savings and loan, that is the place to try first. Set up an appointment with the bank manager or loan officer to make your request and explain why you feel your business venture is worth the bank's investment.

Be aware, however, that banks are more likely to provide you with a loan payable within five or ten years, as opposed to savings and loans, which are more interested in long-term loans, such as for mortgages. Credit unions operate in a similar manner to banks; however, you generally have to be a member. If you do belong to a credit union it could be your best bet, as it offers lower interest rates and can be more flexible in lending decisions.

If, for some reason, you do not want to run a loan through your bank, consider talking with other local small business owners. Very often, they can steer you to a regional, often independently owned bank or savings and loan that is empathetic to and supportive of new businesses. In that case, proceed as

mentioned earlier and arrange a meeting with the manager or loan officer.

Present your case in a friendly yet professional manner. Be realistic and honest about your needs. Do not underbid because you worry that you will not get a loan if you ask for too much. It is always better to start with a higher figure than you actually need so you have a strong negotiating edge.

In addition, most lenders have a pretty good idea about start-up and operating costs of new businesses and are much less likely to give you, and risk losing, a small loan for a business they know calls for more capital. They will be more willing to work with you if you are realistic and knowledgeable about your needs.

> *Money brings some happiness. But, after a certain point, it just brings more money.*
>
> *Neil Simon*

If, after your first try, the answer is no, ask for reasons why you are being turned down so you can restructure your presentation. Turn rejection into a learning tool to redefine and polish your material and to develop new negotiating strategies. There are always other lenders you can approach, and the law of averages dictates that you will get your loan if the idea is solid and it is apparent that you have researched the feasibility of starting a business in your particular area.

Financing Methods

"Friendly Financing"

The third option, raising capital through friends or family members, is probably one of the methods most often used. The advantage of getting a loan from a personal contact is that he or she knows you, undoubtedly trusts your ability to make the business go, and won't require much in the way of substantiating paperwork, such as complex loan applications, financial statements, etc. In addition, you will most likely be able to negotiate a very low interest rate on the loan.

The major disadvantage, according to entrepreneurs who have taken this route, is if the friendly lender decides that he or she wants to provide input on the care and maintenance of your business. This problem, however, can be eliminated by a thorough business discussion prior to accepting the loan. In other words, choose your investor carefully!

The second problem has to do with repayment of the loan. Even though you have a loose agreement in writing with your lender, because of friendship or family ties there may come a point when Uncle Bill needs that $10,000 *tomorrow* to take care of a personal obligation. You can't possibly come up with the money overnight, Uncle Bill gets angry, and that whole side of the family turns against you.

The flip side of the coin is if the business fails and you are unable to pay Uncle Bill the $10,000 he put up. There are any number of unpleasant situations, so you must be sure in the beginning to think about the importance of the relationship you have with the potential lender, how the best and the worst of circumstances would affect your relationship, and whether you then could justify asking for money.

Commercial Lenders

If you are not able to, or if you decide against approaching friends or relatives for financial assistance, the next step is a bank, a savings and loan, or a credit union. Before approaching any of these commercial lenders, you must have carefully developed your business plan, which will include the following documents.

1. A résumé or statement that outlines your employment background and capability to operate the business, plus a similar statement about any key employees or partners in the business

2. A statement of business and personal goals

3. A description of the business, including market research for your product or service

4. Details on how the business is going to be structured (sole proprietorship, partnership, corporation)

5. A projection of profit and loss for a minimum of one year (five years is preferable), which means you will have investigated how similar businesses are doing

6. An outline of how much money you need–and why–to keep the business solvent and to support yourself and your family for at least a year

In addition, you will be required to provide a personal balance sheet that lists your assets (real estate, car, valuable personal property) and liabilities (mortgage payments, credit card debts) along with a credit application that outlines your personal financial history, so a determination can be made on your ability to pay back the loan. The lender will follow through by requesting a credit report from an independent agency to help with the decision.

The main point to remember when applying for a loan with a commercial institution is that lenders aren't as concerned about the amount loaned as they are about how and when they are going to get the money back!

Paying Back the Loan

When you apply for financing, the burden of proof as it relates to repayment rests with you. No one would knowingly grant a loan to an individual or a business that he or she had doubts about. As a borrower, your responsibility is to show that you will be able to pay back the loan according to the terms agreed to by you and the lender. If you have a good credit history, a credit report will indicate as much.

The Small Business Administration

The Small Business Administration (SBA) often goes where no other lender will tread and, as such, is a lender of last resort. The SBA is a government agency that is well known for providing financing to entrepreneurs who have been repeatedly turned down by commercial lenders, which, in fact, you generally must be before the SBA will consider backing you.

After your loan request with a commercial institution has been denied, you can file an application with the nearest branch of the SBA. It is a good idea to make an appointment with a Service

Corps of Retired Executives (SCORE) representative (a man or woman who volunteers his or her time to the SBA-SCORE program to advise new and established business owners). Your SCORE representative will lead you through the complex paperwork required by the SBA before it makes a decision.

In addition, SCORE volunteers are usually straightforward, knowledgeable men and women who will walk through your business plans with you and offer constructive suggestions. Once the paperwork is completed, a commercial lender will make the loan under the SBA Lender Certification Program, knowing that the government is willing to insure it.

We recommend this option only after you have been turned down by three or more banks, because of the time factor involved in gaining approval and also because of the extensive follow-up reports required by the SBA. It is, however, a viable option and one that has helped thousands of dedicated entrepreneurs realize their goals.

Venture Capitalists

Money is available to businesses that are already established and seeking working or expansion capital from groups of investors known as venture capitalists. These groups can vary from a few local businesspeople with some money to invest to major investment companies connected with large corporations or financial organizations.

Venture capital is not like a straightforward business loan. It is usually dependent on a minimum $100,000 investment and, therefore, is not exactly suited to every business situation. Typically, venture capitalists are interested in companies that have a track record, a proven position in the market, and a solid growth projection.

And, like a bank or other lending association, venture capitalists want to see a written business plan and a prospectus of future projections. They are looking at your background, the market, the kind of funding you want, and your past financial record.

Since venture capitalists are looking to earn from 10 to 15 percent on their investment over a relatively short period, they will

want to spend a great deal of time talking with you and your associates, customers, and suppliers.

Before considering venture capital, we advise discussing it carefully with an attorney who can help you investigate different groups to figure out the best investment structure, and who can work with the group's attorney on drawing up an agreement that protects you. Many venture capitalists will want to own part of your company.

This is an option to be considered only when your company is well established and undergoing rapid growth pains and should be approached with great understanding of the situation.

Other Financing Options

Loan Companies

Loan companies are good sources of funding. However, interest rates are high, and they will generally want to have substantial collateral, such as the equity in your house, on record before making a loan.

Insurance Companies

Your insurance carrier may be willing to make an investment in your small business, using your insurance policy as collateral, or you may even have enough cash value in your policy, depending on the face amount, to provide substantial start-up capital. If this is the case, you will only be required to pay quarterly or semiannual interest payments on the cash value you have taken out.

Factoring

In this scenario, a factoring company "buys" your accounts receivable and advances you a percentage of the full amount due. This is a viable option for well-established service companies that work on a billing basis.

Cosigner

If you have a relative or friend who is already an established business owner or, at least, a homeowner with a solid credit rating,

it might be worth your while to ask if he or she would cosign on a loan application with you. Although you are still responsible for repayment of the loan, the bank is assured that, in the event you default for any reason, the cosigner will guarantee the obligation. It is sometimes difficult to find someone who will do this, but again it doesn't hurt to ask, especially if it is a last resort.

Starting Small

Even if you know your particular business is valid and that you have the ability to make it succeed, be certain that your business plan is realistic. If you have chosen to start a business on a grand scale but have minimal capital and little business experience, it may be best to begin a smaller, less elaborate operation at first.

You'll require less "seed money" and will be in a low-risk position while learning the operations of a business and seeing if you can handle all the variables of business ownership while making it grow.

Smaller businesses have proven to be a great way to learn successful methods, as well as a vehicle for ironing out the many small, often overlooked, details. The profits you gain from a smaller venture can be used to expand or invest in bigger business ideas. And an added bonus is that when you are ready to approach investors or lending institutions, you will be able to show them that you already have a solid track record and a working knowledge of business procedures.

The journey of a thousand miles begins with a single step.
Chinese Proverb

What to Do When Asking for Money

1. **Be sure to ask.** This may seem like a gross statement of the obvious, but you would be amazed at the number of small business owners we've heard about who never ask because they are afraid of being turned down.

 Unless you are independently wealthy and pursuing your business as a humanitarian effort, it is unlikely that

you are in a position to run your business and earn enough money to support you, your family, and the operation—especially during the first year. Remember the old adage: It *takes* money to *make* money.

If you run a low-budget business, you will probably get a low-budget response. If you are determined to make it work, be sure you have sufficient capital to make it work the right way.

Fear is often a factor: "I don't want to ask, in case I'm told no." Well, that's the worst thing that can happen. But if you persevere and are serious about your venture, someone will inevitably say yes!

And don't overlook friends and family; they can be your most ardent supporters if you have given them reason in the past to believe you are responsible and determined to succeed.

2. ***Know how much you need.*** Lenders are familiar with the financial demands of business operation and will respect your request if you have obviously done your homework and can talk intelligently about your needs.

3. ***Be direct and confident.*** If you believe in your business and in your ability to make it work, others will be convinced as well. Never apologize for mistakes you feel you have made in the past.

 Simply present the facts honestly, even if it includes revealing an error in judgment you have made somewhere along the line, and assure the lender that he or she will be making a smart decision by investing in you.

4. ***Think positively.*** If you need $50,000, ask for $50,000. Never underestimate the potential to provide. Remember: It is easier to negotiate and deal with one lender for a single amount than it is to keep paperwork and relationships strong with several, all of whom have contributed to the pot.

5. ***Ask again.*** If they trusted you once and you have lived up to the stipulations of the contract, ask again—that goes for commercial lending institutions as well as friends and

relatives. When it comes to borrowing money, a proven record is what it's all about, and if you have established yours, keep it active. It will be your passport to profit when the chips are down.

6. ***Know when to borrow.*** If you have worked out your business plan and know you can survive while getting the business off the ground, start exploring your financing options ahead of time. Don't wait until the last minute when you will be forced to act and will have to take a less-than-favorable opportunity. The same theory applies if your business is already established. By examining your financial position on a regular basis, you will be able to project how much you will need at a given point for expansion purposes. Always be aware.

7. ***Don't borrow if it is not necessary.*** Many businesses can be started for under $1,000. This is called "starting on a shoestring" and can be done with a variety of businesses. Services, for example, often rely strictly on the owner's knowledge and expertise and can be set up quickly and inexpensively.

 If this is the case with the business you have in mind, then try to avoid borrowing money, which can be an expensive and timely proposition.

Establishing Credit

Is it possible to get a loan even if you have never established credit? Yes, it is. If you prefer to pay cash rather than incur high interest charges on loans or credit cards, you can still qualify for a loan based on personal assets or by having a friend or relative with a good credit rating cosign for you on the loan. This puts the obligation on the cosigner, so be sure the terms of the loan are clearly spelled out in a written agreement to the satisfaction of everyone involved.

But, if your personal assets are minimal and you cannot find a cosigner, your best bet is to put off starting the business for four to six months while you establish credit. The best place to start is with a major department store. A store will issue you a credit card

based on a very simple examination of your income and employment history. When you receive the card, charge about $100 worth of merchandise and pay it off according to the schedule provided. Within a few months, you will have proven yourself to be credit worthy, which will greatly improve your chances of getting a loan from a lending institution.

Another way to establish credit—and credibility—is to open a checking account at the bank you have decided to approach for a loan. Banks generally require a minimum deposit of between $50 and $100. Make it a point to meet the branch manager and/or the loan officer and establish an ongoing relationship with them by stopping by to say hello when you are in the bank.

Within a few months, apply for a small personal loan, working with your new acquaintance, of course. Make your payments according to the prearranged schedule. Then when you are ready to request a more substantial amount of money to cover your start-up expenses, you will be recognized as a customer with a loan history at that institution.

Notes

Key Points

Personal Thoughts

Additional Research

15

RECORD KEEPING: YOUR
BUSINESS LIFELINE

The motivating factor in any business is profit, which can be explained as the money left over after all the bills—everything from supplies to rent to salaries to taxes—are paid.

Building a profitable business is not something that can be left to chance; it must be planned, and a systematic method of record keeping must be developed to help you monitor income and expenses.

You should expect that during the early days of your business, your profits are going to be minimal as you become established. But it is possible, with even simple record-keeping procedures, to prepare yourself for lean periods and control day-to-day expenses to ensure that you are, at least, breaking even. In addition, financial records are required for tax purposes, and dealing with them systematically can help you avoid an incredibly overwhelming task at tax time.

Record Keeping Can Be Simple

Some people cringe at the thought of record keeping or feel it is a waste of valuable time. Usually, these attitudes are based on a lack of knowledge and the feeling that it is a difficult job. There is, however, no other way to analyze your cash flow and make sure you are pricing products or services high enough to realize a profit.

In truth, record keeping is not a complicated process. If you have ever balanced a checkbook or planned a household budget, you have performed several of the same steps that are necessary for implementing a bookkeeping system for your business. And the good news is that keeping business records does not have to be either complicated or time-consuming.

We know of entrepreneurs who opt for total simplicity by using the "shoebox" method—every sales record, receipt for expenses, and bank statement gets tossed into a box. This system has two distinct drawbacks. One may not become apparent until tax time, when you attempt to wade through and organize each sheet of paper to prepare your tax return. The other, more critical drawback is that it is virtually impossible to maintain an accurate picture of your financial situation when you stockpile, rather than record, business transactions.

In order to understand your cash flow, it is important to be able to see monies earned, monies paid out, current balances, and outstanding debts.

In fact, you should be able to answer the following questions with just a quick review of your records.

♦ What was my income last year (week, month)?

♦ What were my expenses?

♦ How do income and expenses compare with last year (week, month)?

♦ What was my profit (loss) last year (week, month)?

♦ Where can I cut back on expenses?

♦ Who and how much do I currently owe on outstanding debts?

♦ Who owes me money and how much?

♦ What are my assets, liabilities, and net worth?

♦ Is my inventory in line with demand?

♦ How much cash do I have available? How much credit?

♦ Am I able to pay myself this month (week)?

♦ Are my figures in line with projected financial goals?

The records you need to be able to answer most of these questions are your cash journal, a balance sheet, and a bank reconciliation. A simple single-entry system, as indicated on the following pages, where you can record disbursements (cash paid out) and receipts (cash taken in) will form the base of your record-keeping system.

> *If you can organize your kitchen, you can organize your life.*
>
> Dr. Louis Parrish

Double-Entry Bookkeeping

You may want to consider a double-entry system, which involves recording each transaction twice; once as a debit (simply the left column of the ledger) and once as a credit (the right column of the ledger). For example, if you were to sell a product for $100, the transactions recorded in a double-entry system would be as follows: The $100 would be written as a *credit* in your sales account, since merchandise is going out of the business, and $100 would be recorded as a *debit* in your cash account since money was coming into the business.

This is a complex and time-consuming process that is often best left to an accountant, as he or she will need the information to create a monthly trial balance and other financial statements, including your year-end tax reports.

Bookkeeping Debits and Credits

Debits

◆ Cash receipts

◆ Purchases

◆ Expenses, such as rent and wages

Credits

◆ Cash payments

◆ Sales of services or merchandise

◆ Earnings, including interest

Single-Entry Bookkeeping

You can, however, set up a simple single-entry system, which will tie in directly with your accountant's requirements, or check out the standardized bookkeeping systems available at office supply or stationery stores, which provide all the necessary forms and documents in a bound book.

A system should contain forms for recording monthly income and expenses, summary sheets from which you can create a balance sheet, and listings of legal deductions for income tax reporting. In addition, the trade association for your field should be able to provide you with systems developed exclusively for use in the industry, which you can use or adapt according to the specific circumstances of your business.

The final method is to purchase a cash journal book and set up your own monthly system. (We've used Office Assistance, a small secretarial service that has been in operation for one month, as an example.) Any of the above-mentioned methods are acceptable, as long as you understand the entry process and can read the results.

Make Record Keeping a Daily Task

Short of paying someone else, the easiest way to be sure your records are kept up-to-date is to incorporate the task into your daily or weekly routine. Many small business owners make it a habit to enter their sales, expenses, and other financial information at the end of each working day. It keeps them continually aware of their financial situation and ensures that there will never be any cash-flow surprises.

The process shouldn't take more than fifteen minutes for normal transactions, and it will save hours of pencil pushing and frustration down the line. What's important is that you'll always know where you stand financially.

Setting Up the Books

Now, using the fictitious Office Assistance as an example, we will examine the various elements required for basic record-keeping duties.

Office Assistance has been in business for one month. Two months ago, Bill Miller, president of Office Assistance, opened a new business bank account with $10,000, his start-up capital from a personal savings account.

At the same time, he rented a small office in a downtown building for $350 a month, but had to pay the first month's rent, and a deposit of the last month's rent, for a total outlay of $700.

His fictitious name statement, which he got approved through the local county clerk's office, cost $10, and publishing it in a regional newspaper cost $45.

The initial month's lease and a deposit on a computer cost him $275, plus $50 for a maintenance agreement. However, he will own the $2,000 computer when his payment schedule is completed.

He found a brand-new calculator at a garage sale for $25 and is going to use a desk, table, lamp, and chairs brought from home (value $350) to decorate the office. Phone-line installation was $150, and he purchased a two-line telephone for $79.50.

An artist friend designed his logo and letterhead on a computer for only $25 and a $6.95 lunch. He had his stationery ($35),

business cards ($60), and brochures ($23.50) produced through a local copy shop for a total of $118.50.

A 2 x 2-inch display ad in the local newspaper will cost him $370 for a week, and he is planning to mail 100 of his brochures to local businesses selected from the phone book. Stamps will cost $32 for the mailing. Office supplies, including typing paper, staples, paper clips, etc., set him back $45. A journal for record keeping cost $7.95 and a packet of invoices $5.95, for a grand total of $58.90.

Since he doesn't know how to type, Bill hired his niece to work 20 hours a week for $10 per hour on an independent contractor basis so he doesn't have to pay social security or unemployment taxes.

During the first month, he has billed and been paid $700. However, he has two clients who still owe him a total of $400. Bill dutifully records information in his cash journal at the end of each working day. He uses source documents, including his checkbook register, receipts from cash purchases, and billing invoices as the basis for his entries. The following cash journal illustrations are for May (prior to opening the doors of his business) and June (his first actual month in business).

Bill's expenses for May and June were $3,108.75. Of course, part of that is for start-up expenses, such as deposits on his rent and computer, installation costs, and one-time fictitious name filing and publishing. His income for the first month was $700.

Office Assistance
Cash Journal for May

Date	Check # or Invoice #	Detail	(Debit) Expense	(Credit) Income
5/1	100	Rawlins Real Estate (rent & dep)	$700.00	
5/5	101	County Clerk (fictitious name)	10.00	
5/7	102	The Herald (publishing FNS)	45.00	
5/9	103	Ed's Keyboards (IBM l-mo. & dep)	275.00	
5/9	104	Ed's Keyboards (maint. agreement)	50.00	
5/12	105	Mary Smith (calculator purchase)	25.00	
5/18	106	Telephone Co. (line installation)	150.00	
5/20	107	Phone Store (2-line phone)	79.50	
5/22	108	Ray Brown (logo design)	25.00	
5/24	Cash	The Hungry Dog (lunch/Ray Brown)	6.95	
5/28	109	The Copy Spot (brochures, cards)	118.50	
5/29	110	The Herald (advertising)	370.00	
		Total Expense & Income (May)	$1,854.95	$00.00

Office Assistance
Cash Journal for June

Date	Check # or Invoice #	Detail	(Debit) Expense	(Credit) Income
6/4	111	U.S.P.O. (stamps for mailing)	$29.00	
6/6	112	Office Stationers (supplies, invoices, etc.)	58.90	
6/7	A1	W. Smith		$62.50
6/8	A2	Art Association		112.50
6/9	A3	T. Williams		22.00
6/9	113	Judy Miller (typing fee)	200.00	
6/10	A4	Bank of Cutterville		75.00
6/10	A5	WKTR-FM		120.50
6/13	A6	J. Johnson		43.50
6/15	114	Rawlins Real Estate (rent)	350.00	
6/15	A7	C. Lewis		73.50
6/15	A8	R. Swell		90.00
6/16	115	Judy Miller (typing fee)	200.00	
6/19	A9	W. Smith		52.50
6/23	116	Judy Miller (typing fee)	200.00	
6/26	117	Phone company (bill)	15.90	
6/27	A10	K. Black		48.00
6/30	118	Judy Miller (typing fee)	200.00	
		Total Expense & Income (June)	**$1,253.80**	**$700.00**

Balance Sheet (as of June 30)

Assets		Liabilities	
Cash on hand & in bank *(Capital balance & June income)*	$6,191.25	Ed's Keyboards *(Balance on IBM)* Unpaid rent *(July)*	$1,725.00 350.00
Office equipment *(Includes full value of IBM even though not paid off)*	2,000.00	Taxes *(estimated)*	75.00
Office furniture	350.00		
Accounts receivable *(Outstanding invoices for work already done)*	400.00	**Liabilities**	**$2,150.00**
Total Assets	**$8,941.25**	**CAPITAL**	**$6,791.25**
		Total Liabilities	**$8,941.25**

By deducting his expenses from his income, he can see that, at the moment, his business is showing a loss of $2,408.75.

Although Bill has only been in business for a month, he is curious about his company's financial worth and decides to work up a balance sheet to get the answer. The calculation, as indicated in the example, is the amount owned (assets) minus the amount due to creditors (liabilities), which equals his worth.

The figure Bill is most interested in is the CAPITAL amount in the Liabilities column. This is the amount remaining after what Bill owes is subtracted from his current assets and is what his business is worth at the end of June. In other words, if he decided to try to sell his business right now, he could realistically ask that amount as a selling price. Of course, Bill probably wouldn't get that amount because he has not yet become established enough to warrant someone buying the business, unless he or she was looking for a "turnkey" operation—in other words, a business to just walk into and get going immediately.

This information is valuable when Bill goes to apply for expansion capital or for credit on future purchases he plans to make. His balance sheet will change each time he prepares it (probably quarterly in the future) as business improves, bringing in greater income and reducing his debts.

In the meantime, the balance sheet gives Bill a tool to use when comparing the financial standing of his business this month against future months and years. It also keeps him current on what he owns, to whom he owes money, and his major sources of income.

The same procedure is used in developing a personal balance sheet, which possibly would be needed to establish credibility when applying for a loan. Assets would include furniture, automobiles, jewelry, a home, and other tangibles, while liabilities would consist of outstanding loans and other major debts.

Bank Statement Reconciliation

Another important step that Bill must handle monthly is reconciling his bank statement against his checkbook register. He simply marks off the checks in his register that have cleared per the bank statement, notes the deposits that have been credited, and deducts any service charges for the previous month from his balance.

Bill then adds up all the outstanding checks–those listed in his register that have not cleared by the closing date indicated on the bank statement–and *deducts* them from the balance indicated on his bank statement. He adds up any deposits that have not yet been credited to his account and then *adds* them to the balance, as follows.

Balance per bank statement	$5,982.15
Plus: Deposits not credited	+325.00
Minus: Outstanding checks	-115.90
New Balance	$ 6,191.25

The new balance figure should match that listed in his checkbook register and, in this case, it does. If, however, the statement and the register did not reconcile, Bill would have a customer representative at the bank review his statement and banking activity for the past month.

The Catering Work Order

The records specific to your catering business can essentially be handled by an all-purpose contract, which serves as a work order, invoice, and sales receipt all in one package. Be diligent about using the contracts and keeping copies on file in some organized way, so you'll have all the information you need at your fingertips. Don't forget to keep copies of invoices for food and other supplies with the contracts for each job.

Notes

Key Points

Personal Thoughts

Additional Research

16

PRICING FOR PROFITS

One of the toughest problems that small business owners face is establishing prices that the market will bear but that will also cover overhead and guarantee a profit.

Too often, new business owners give away business to get sales. Realistic pricing indicates your confidence in your service or product; if you value it, so will the customer.

Today's consumers realize that they can't get something worthwhile for nothing, so don't be afraid to establish prices that will work toward your profit goals.

Guidelines

Several factors must be taken into consideration when setting prices:

1. *The cost of goods sold.* In the case of a retail or wholesale operation, this is the amount originally paid for the goods. For a manufacturer, it is the cost of producing the goods.

2. *The nature of the product or service.* Uniqueness and demand come into play here. In the case of goods with a stable level of demand, such as bread or auto repair,

raising or lowering prices will have little effect. However, when demand is high for goods that are hard to get, the price can realistically be set anywhere the business owner wants. Such is often the case with restaurants featuring an exclusive or unusual menu.

3. ***The competition.*** It is important to recognize what your competition is charging, for often this will guide pricing within a certain region. However, if a competitor is charging what you feel is an unrealistic price—either more or less—for a product or service, you owe it to yourself to find out why. Then set your prices according to all of the factors outlined here. Even if your prices are higher than the competitor, consumers will pay the cost if you offer something special, such as a friendly atmosphere, convenient hours, follow-up service or maintenance, or some other benefit not provided by the competition.

4. ***Your company policy.*** This encompasses a number of things, including your location, your position in the marketplace, and additional services offered. It also takes into account your personal philosophy about business and your role in it.

5. ***Market strategy.*** Should you go for large volume at low prices or low volume at high prices? That is the bottom line in considering market strategy. As a small business owner, you will likely opt for low volume and higher prices, since the alternative involves having the resources, including labor, display room, distribution channels, etc., to move large volumes of product or perform major service tasks.

6. ***Customers.*** What will the market bear? In other words, what are your customers willing to pay for your products or services?

People expect prices that are fair; if you are planning to charge overinflated rates you had better be a topnotch salesperson or have something so incredible and unusual to offer that the price won't matter.

Although there are differences between establishing prices for retail operations, wholesale products, manufacturing, and services, the basic formula for price setting is

Labor + Materials + Overhead + Profit Margin = Price

However, before setting prices on goods or services, it is extremely important to understand the concept of the break-even point. Many small business owners operate on an overall profit-loss basis without realizing the importance of cost accounting. Being aware of such factors as your break-even point, markup, and profit margin can tell you which areas of your business are profitable and which are causing a drain.

Understanding Break-even

The break-even point is the minimum amount you must charge in order to cover all expenses incurred for the production and promotion of your goods and/or services *without losing or making money.* In other words, any income that is above the break-even point is considered to be profit and anything below it is a loss.

To find your break-even point, you must first total all of your operating costs, including materials and labor, equipment lease or purchase payments, advertising, utilities, office supplies, and any incidentals such as gasoline, maintenance, and postage.

Generally, this is computed for a particular period of time, such as six months or a year. However, if your business is still in the early stages of operation, you can use the estimated figures on your projected expense statement and guesstimate costs for materials and labor.

For example, the monthly expenses for your hypothetical cake-decorating business total $300. You want to know what the break-even point would be if you sold an average of 20 cakes per month. The calculation is as follows:

$$\frac{\$300 \text{ (expenses)}}{20 \text{ cakes}} = \$15.00$$

In order to break even, that is, to operate without losing money or realizing a profit, you must charge a minimum of $15 for each cake sold.

The same process can be used to analyze the break-even point on a weekly basis. First you determine your annual expenses by multiplying the $300 by 12 months, which would give you $3,600 per year.

The calculation to find the weekly break-even point follows:

$$\frac{\$3,600 \text{ (expenses)}}{52 \text{ weeks}} = \$69.23$$

Therefore, you must earn $69.23 per week to operate the business without losing money and without realizing a profit.

Stay Informed

Knowing your break-even point is one of the greatest favors you can do for yourself as a business owner. It tells you how much you must charge for your products or services and is invaluable in setting prices to realize a profit.

Keep in mind, however, that the break-even point is a variable figure. Since it depends on production and overhead costs, plan to reevaluate periodically to make sure your prices reflect any changes.

Labor Costs

Labor costs, obviously, are the expenses incurred for the actual work done to manufacture or sell a product or to perform a service. Think of them as wages or salaries.

Small business owners often end up working for free because they fail to set a wage for themselves. Despite the fact that you will want to reinvest all of the income received back into the business for a while, it is imperative that you establish a fixed salary amount for yourself when figuring operating expenses.

If you have set aside a survival fund to carry you through the first six months of operation, you may want to defer your salary until the business becomes solvent; however, you should still figure the amount into your expenses. Otherwise, you may find the prices you set are too low to justify making a profit from the onset.

It is much easier to set realistic prices from the beginning than it is to raise them later in an attempt to make up the difference. Remember, your time and skills are the cornerstone of your business, so think of paying yourself as you would any valuable employee.

Setting Retail Prices

If you are manufacturing items to sell at retail prices, without using a middleman, use the following formula as a starting point when establishing a selling price for your inventory of goods.

$$\frac{1}{3} \text{ Labor} + \frac{1}{3} \text{ Materials \& Overhead} + \frac{1}{3} \text{ Profit} = \text{Selling Price}$$

You need a foundation. One place to start is with your labor costs. If, for example, the monetary value of your time and effort (labor) in producing an item was $6, you would allocate $6 for material, $6 for overhead and an additional $6 as profit for a total selling price of $18.

If materials and overhead are costing more, you can (a) boost the price accordingly; (b) review your expenses and find ways to

cut back on material costs, such as finding a less expensive supplier; or (c) utilize a portion of the profit margin to cover the balance. Of the three options, (b) is the best way to go.

You must also remember that when you are producing mass quantities of an item, your costs will be reduced because of price breaks on supplies and reduced labor costs per unit. You're then able to structure your selling price according to previously mentioned pricing factors, such as competition and demand for the product.

Money is the sixth sense which makes it possible for us to enjoy the other five senses.

Richard Ney

If you are starting a retail business that relies on selling products you purchase wholesale, you may have some of your prices set for you by what the competition is doing, or by recommendations made by the wholesaler. However, there will still be items you must price yourself.

This will involve understanding the principle of markup or gross margin—the difference between the cost of goods sold and the selling price, taking into consideration sale markdowns, shortages, and discounts to employees. Generally, markup is stated as a percentage of retail price.

For example, if a manufacturer sells dresses to you at a wholesale price of $12.50 each and you sell them for $25, you would have a 100 percent markup (a 50 percent gross margin).

If you know the cost of goods and the average amount of markup you need to operate profitably, it is relatively simple to determine a price by using the following formula:

$$\frac{\text{Cost of goods}}{100 - \text{markup \%} \times 100} = \text{Retail Price}$$

For example, if you purchased a gross of rubber ducks for a total price of $172.80 and had determined that you needed a gross margin of 36 percent to operate profitably, you would calculate the expected profit as follows:

$$\frac{\$172.80}{100 - 36 \times 100} = \$270$$

When you divide the retail price ($270) by the number of items in a gross (12 dozen or 144 things) you get a unit price of $1.88, which you would probably raise to $1.98, depending on the market, to improve the profit margin slightly and provide leeway for markdowns during sales, etc.

Specialty items, such as antiques, artwork, imported goods, and handcrafted items can be priced higher according to current value and what the market in your area will bear. Their markup usually ranges between 200 and 300 percent.

Setting Wholesale Prices

Operating as a wholesale manufacturer greatly reduces your selling and administrative costs, because you are passing your products on to someone else to sell. Your price to retailers should thus be approximately 50 percent less than the suggested retail price.

In actuality, you are providing retailers with a discount because of their willingness and ability to promote your product.

The formula for wholesale pricing includes your profit margin + labor costs + expenses, which will be appreciably lower than for a retail operation because of savings on advertising, display equipment, and maintenance, but which must include warehousing and marketing.

Pricing is typically more competitive at the wholesale level than at any other and is almost always the determining factor in whether your products are purchased or not.

Also affecting wholesalers are other wholesalers offering competitive pricing, middlemen buying large quantities at low prices, and supply and demand factors.

As a wholesaler, you are in a position to vary prices according to the size of orders and your ability to negotiate with buyers. However, it is a good idea to develop a solid markup base from which to operate. This will allow you the flexibility to offer maximum and minimum prices for each item based on quantity buys.

Pricing is a crucial aspect of managing your business. Since you are in business to make a profit, it is important that you set prices that will result in the greatest income.

Catering Rates

Before establishing prices, it is essential to have an accurate picture of all costs. This includes costs for raw food materials, transportation, preparation and serving time, and overhead expenses (fixed and variable).

Food costs should be broken down by recipe; assess every ingredient from salt and pepper to primary ingredients such as meat and vegetables. This analysis may seem tedious, but it is the most accurate way of knowing the exact cost of each menu item. When planning a menu, keep the cost analysis in mind, and try to strike a balance between expensive and inexpensive offerings.

Costing Out Food Supplies

Figuring cost on primary ingredients will be easy, because it will, in most cases, be the same amount charged by the supplier. When ordering for more than one job at the same time, ask for separate invoices from the supplier so you can accurately assess costs for each job.

To figure the cost of items such as salt and other spices, find out how many servings there are per container. For example, a standard 26-ounce container of salt contains 55 ⅓ tablespoons. (Equivalent measurements for liquid and dry ingredients are listed in most major cookbooks.)

Therefore, if the container costs 75 cents and you use 2 ⅛ tablespoons (1 ounce) of salt in your recipe, you can list this ingredient at 3 cents. It may seem trivial, but those pennies add up over a period of time.

Spend some time creating a cost-analysis chart for frequently-used items such as sugar, flour, vanilla, and eggs. Break out the costs by typical measurements (per cup or per tablespoon, for example).

Although some food costs change depending on the season or supplier, it should not be difficult to figure an average cost for most ingredients.

Pricing Methods

Once the costs have been assessed, there are several standard pricing methods that can be employed. One option is to figure estimated total cost, add 10 percent to cover unexpected expenses, and divide the sum by the number of guests.

Cost of goods & overhead: $500.00
Number of guests: 35

$$\frac{\text{Cost of goods}}{\text{guests}} = \$14.29$$
(rounded off to $14.50)

Then add 15 percent to the total to cover your projected profit, which gives you the base price per guest to the client:

$14.50 + 15% profit = $16.75
($2.17 rounded off to $2.25)

An even simpler method is to charge three times the cost of food, which will work well for small functions, as long as you don't have a lot of other major expenses, such as wages, floral arrangements, or rental fees for expensive serving equipment.

Cost of food = $145.00 x 3 = $435.00

Divide the final amount by the number of attendees to get the price per guest.

In order to find out if you are within the projected budgetary guidelines determined by you and your accountant, break down your costs on a straight percentage basis. Basing the sample equation on a per-guest price of $16.50, it is possible to find out exactly how you are doing by using the following percentages:

Cost of Food 25%
Preparation & Serving Time 25%
Overhead 20%
Profit 30%

These are average percentages assessed by many caterers and will serve as a starting point for budgeting. Your accountant can help you work out percentages that are customized to your situation and that take into consideration such variables as the expense of a commercial location versus a home-based kitchen, full-time versus part-time employees, and money spent on advertising and promotion.

Creating a Price List

Once you have a repertoire of recipes, establish a price list to help clients decide on their menu.

Price List Sample

Menu Selection

Quiche Lorraine, Salmon Steak w/Dijon Mustard
Sauce, Sage Butter Noodles, Baby Carrots and
Snow Peas **$9.50 per serving**

Stuffed Mushrooms, Baked Chicken Curry,
Wild Rice Almondine, Veggie Kabobs **$8.25 per serving**

Roast Beef Open Face Sandwich, Mashed Potatoes,
Pasta Salad, Apple Sauce Boats **$7.50 per serving**

Keep in mind that expenses decrease as the number of guests increases because of discounts for quantity purchases and the reduced preparation time for certain items. Passing along these savings to your clients will give you a reputation as a fair-minded caterer. An amended price list might look like this:

Price List Example

Menu Selection	*Per Serving Price*		
	10-25	26-75	76+
Quiche Lorraine, Salmon Steak w/ Dijon Mustard Sauce, Sage Butter Noodles, Baby Carrots and Snow Peas	$9.50	$9.00	$8.75
Stuffed Mushrooms, Baked Chicken Curry, Wild Rice Almondine, Veggie Kabobs	$8.25	$8.00	$7.50
Roast Beef Open Face Sandwich, Mashed Potatoes, Pasta Salad, Apple Sauce Boats	$7.50	$7.25	$6.50

Remember to include a written statement that prices are subject to change. This will allow you to adjust for increases in food costs and overhead. When you must raise prices across the board, however, create a new price list as soon as possible.

Clients will not take kindly to paying more than what you have printed on your price list. For this reason, and to ensure that all costs are covered, most caterers prefer to give an original estimate for each job. Other pricing factors to consider are:

The type of service being provided. Catering a cocktail party is far easier than catering a wedding reception. The cocktail party might be billed at approximately $5.00 per person while the reception could run $50.00 or more per person.

Time. It is acceptable in the catering business to add a premium for high-profit holiday assignments or unusual requests, such as an after-theater dinner scheduled to begin at 10:30 p.m.

The client. As a gesture of goodwill, consider offering steady customers a small courtesy discount. It will pay for itself by assuring you repeat business and by saving time (given your familiarity with the needs of these clients, initial meetings will be brief).

Budget. A large corporation hosting an employee bash probably has a bigger budget than a family hosting a birthday party. Use common sense in establishing fees for various situations and occasions.

Your reputation. As word of your talent spreads, business will grow appreciably. As a result, you are justified in raising your rates.

Employee considerations. When budgeting for a job, you may want to include a gratuity for your serving staff. Fifteen percent is standard. Although many clients will offer a higher gratuity when they pay you—especially if they are pleased with the food and the service—you can make sure employees are properly compensated by building the tip into the fee.

YOUR CATERING COMPANY

1 Main Street 555-5555

Invoice for Catering Services

To: _____ Date: _____

Buffet for 200 guests held at 1234 City Street
per contract signed and dated _____

200 guests @ $10.00	$2,000.00

Additional charges:

Floral arrangements	300.00
Wedding cake	70.00
Sub-Total	$2,370.00
Less Deposit	$1,000.00
Balance Due	**$1,370.00**

Thank You. We look forward to serving you again.

Developing the Quote

One of the few firm rules in catering is to never give a quote over the telephone. You may grossly underbid the job and then be held to an unrealistic and unfair price.

Meet with the client in person and write down every detail of what they want, from specific food selections to additional services, such as a bartender or special uniforms for the serving staff. You can then suggest options for making their function special and memorable. After the meeting, analyze the information and draw up a contract.

Let the dining-room be well lighted, the cloth impeccably white...Let the dishes be few in number, but exquisitely chosen...Let the service (of these dishes) proceed from the most substantial to the lightest...

Brillat-Savarin

The main points to cover with the client are: occasion, location, time, number of guests, type of service, and food preferences.

Occasion

For a birthday party, the client may prefer a buffet or a formal sit-down meal. A lunchtime business meeting typically calls for a variety of salads and cold cuts. And light entrees or an ethnic cuisine are appropriate for a pre-theater gathering.

Location

If possible, meet the client at the place where the event will be held. This will give you the opportunity to inspect the kitchen and serving areas. Review with the client how tables are to be arranged and check access for loading and unloading.

If you are going to be preparing and cooking on-site, make sure the appliances (stove, refrigerator, etc.) work and are large enough to accommodate the menu. Check to see if there is a dishwasher available. Also inspect the quality and quantity of cookware and serving dishes.

Time

Clients may be unsure about what meal to serve at a particular time of day. Use the following as a standard guideline:

Breakfast	6 a.m. to approx. 11 a.m.
Brunch	1 a.m. to 1 p.m. *(2 p.m. on Sunday)*
Lunch	11:30 a.m. to 2:30 p.m.
Tea	11:30 a.m. to 4:30 p.m.
Cocktails	Anytime after 4:30 p.m.
Dinner	5:30 to 10:00 p.m.
Late Supper	Anytime after 10:00 p.m.

Once the client has decided what time food will be served, develop your "start-to-finish" schedule. Estimate how long it will take to accomplish the following tasks:

◆ Food shopping and preparation

◆ Travel time to and from the function

◆ Loading and unloading food and supplies

◆ Setting up tables, serving areas and decorations

◆ Reheating and arranging food on serving trays or plates

◆ Serving time from hors d'oeuvres to the final cup of coffee

◆ Dining area clean-up

◆ Kitchen clean-up

The estimated "start-to-finish" time should be documented in the contract, along with the hours that the room or location will be available for your use. The client should be able to provide this information. If, however, the client is renting space in a banquet

room or social hall, the burden may be on you to contact the management for details.

Type and Number of Guests

This is an important factor in setting your price and in planning the menu. If the group is small, the client probably knows the guests and can give you an idea of their culinary preferences and adventurousness. In this case, you may want to recommend more unusual selections in the gourmet or ethnic categories.

On the other hand, if the group is large and diverse—for example, a wedding reception with guests of various ages and backgrounds—you may want to suggest a more universally appealing menu.

Food Preferences

Ask the client if there are any dietary restrictions or food preferences you should be aware of when designing the menu. Be prepared to suggest menu items that are aligned with religious guidelines, diabetic restrictions, low-calorie or sodium-free requirements, vegetarian preferences, and children's palates (small portions, non-spicy foods).

Catering Tips

◆ Take time to develop unique menus for different occasions and celebrations.

◆ Review recipes and test them several times to make sure you know them well.

◆ Study the major cookbooks, which offer complete menu suggestions which you can adapt to clients needs.

Service Requirements

People tend to serve themselves larger portions at a buffet table than would be served to them on a plate at a sit-down dinner. When

contracting a buffet event, make allowances for more food purchasing and preparation.

Additional Services

Some clients expect caterers to arrange for musicians, a photographer, flowers, and even the printing of invitations or announcements for a function. Decide in advance whether you have the time and interest in providing full party or event planning.

If so, do not hesitate to charge more money—generally a percent of the fees established by those providing the additional service. If you decide against contracting outside services, simply tell the client that your specialty is food catering, and offer to direct them to someone who can help with extended planning.

Prepare a list of referrals from the telephone book or from other caterers in your area. It is a good idea to talk with the individual musicians, photographers, florists, and printers so that you know what they offer and how much they charge.

After your initial fact-finding meeting, calculate the figures and draw up a contract that covers all of the details outlined above, as well as any specifics requested by the client. This contract can be written out in a letter or in a standardized form. Make three copies of the contract—one for the client, one to be signed and returned to you, and one additional copy for the job envelope.

Also outline the payment schedule in the contract. It is customary practice to require 50 percent of the fee as an advance deposit to cover your immediate expenses. Payment of the remaining 50 percent can be requested immediately following the event (after the guests leave and before you start clean-up chores) or within a specified period of time (no more than two weeks after the event). When writing the invoice for the balance due, use the information from the contract.

Cancellations

Nothing is more annoying to a caterer than a last-minute cancellation. For this reason, it is important to include in the contract a cancellation clause that outlines your policy. Typically, a percentage (or all) of the deposit is retained by the caterer. In some cases,

of course, the cancellation is due to unforeseen and inescapable circumstances (such as serious illness or death). These situations, which are often tragic and unavoidable, call for a more lenient cancellation policy. Use good judgment to determine how much of the deposit should be returned to the client. Unacceptable reasons for cancellation include "personal reasons" that the client won't discuss, a sudden lack of funds, or a change of heart on the part of the bride or groom.

If Clients Don't Pay

If you are firm about your payment schedule from the outset, the majority of clients (90 percent, according to most caterers) will pay the balance according to your expectations. This is especially true if you make it a policy to collect payment immediately after the event. If, however, a customer is slow-paying or withholds payment, you have several avenues of recourse.

The first step is to send a personal letter reminding the client of the amount due and requesting payment within a reasonable period of time (10 days is considered reasonable). State that you realize the client may have forgotten about the bill, even if you know they haven't. In other words, give them the benefit of the doubt. In most cases, this will result in immediate payment.

Getting Tough

Next, call the client or make a personal visit to his or her home or office. Explain that you provided services in good faith and have expenses which necessitate your getting paid. If this doesn't elicit a check or promise of payment in the very near future, tell the client that you will be forced to take further action.

Ask your lawyer to send a standard collection letter on his or her letterhead. This tactic is usually effective in getting the client to remit payment, but it will cost you—probably your attorney's hourly charge.

Last Resorts

Small claims court

If your attempts are not successful, consider taking the client to small claims court. Although this process takes time, it is inexpensive. Claims are limited to a certain amount (anywhere from $1,200 to $2,000 depending on which state you live in). There are two things to keep in mind when taking someone to small claims court:

1. Judgment may not be made in your favor. Depending on how the judge weighs both sides of the story, you may lose the amount due as well as the time and money invested in filing the claim.

2. Even if the judgment is made in your favor, there is no guarantee that you will receive immediate payment. The client may continue to hold back payment, or may claim in court that he or she is under financial duress.

Collection agencies

These agencies take a percentage, often a large one, of the final payment collected. They hound the client and send threatening letters indicating how the client's credit rating will be affected by refusal to pay the bill. Sometimes this tactic works and sometimes it doesn't.

"Creative collection" has proven successful for many people. One caterer, who was owed $2,000 by a lawyer for a party she catered, "camped out" in the lobby of his office. After she voluntarily informed two of his waiting clients the reason she was there, he authorized his perplexed secretary to pay the full amount due. This measure can be time-consuming and even risky, but if you or a hardy friend have the fortitude to try it, it could be the answer!

Notes

Key Points

Personal Thoughts

Additional Research

17

INVENTORY AS INVESTMENT

Ask 100 small business owners what inventory means to them and more than 90 percent will tell you it's the merchandise they keep on hand to sell to their customers, or the materials and supplies stocked to produce goods or perform a service.

This is somewhat accurate, for inventory can and should be viewed as any supplies, raw materials, or finished goods used to generate a profit in your business. But it isn't the response that a savvy business owner would give.

Surprisingly, according to a recent study conducted by a leading consulting firm, less than 10 percent of a group of 500 entrepreneurs interviewed spoke of their inventory in terms of the *investment it represents*; an investment that can range from 15 to 25 percent of total operating capital.

It is because of this misunderstanding that many small business owners often fail to incorporate good inventory control practices into their regular management routine. Although they keep an eagle eye on every penny going through the books, they may totally overlook the cash tied up in their inventory.

Controlling Inventory

Inventory control can be a very simple, straightforward task if you implement a workable system from the beginning—preferably even *before* you start ordering and receiving goods. You will find that time really flies when you are self-employed, and it's very easy to postpone such tasks as inventory control until the inevitable day you find yourself facing this overwhelming job. Inventory control will give you valuable information about: (a) whether or not you are carrying too much or too little inventory based on, for example, items and prices preferred by your customers, or seasonal aspects, and (b) if you are realizing optimum economy determined by the costs of storage, taxes, handling, and the investment per unit.

> *Although there are countless alumni of the school of hard knocks, there has not yet been a move to accredit that institution.*
>
> Sonya Rudikoff

The ideal situation is to maintain an inventory that is profitable because it turns over (comes in and goes out of the business) regularly, thereby lowering the cost of storing, displaying, and insuring it.

There are several methods of inventory control that you can adopt, depending on your business. The main goal with each method, however, is to tell you how many items you have on hand and how many you need to meet your customer or production demands. It will also work toward lessening inventory shrinkage, which is generally the result of employee pilferage; customer theft; incorrect inventory storage; or sloppy record maintenance of items ordered, received, and used.

You can tell how many items you currently have by making an educated guess, which generally only works for businesses having a small, visible inventory that is relatively predictable. An example of the kind of business that could probably operate efficiently with this relaxed form of inventory control would be a one- or two-person enterprise that monthly goes through a box of invoices and similar supplies available for a minimum amount at the discount office-supply store.

Other methods of inventory control are *the physical count*, which should be done at least once a year for tax purposes, or—the easiest and most efficient of them all—*an ongoing* record. Ideally, you should incorporate both systems by backing up periodic physical counts with a perpetual record.

To set up your perpetual system, simply create a file card or inventory sheet in a three-ring binder for each item in your inventory. Across the top of the card or sheet, list the following:

1. Item name and code number, if applicable
2. A description of the item
3. Where it is stored
4. The supplier's name, address, and phone number
5. Unit price (i.e., $12.95/dozen)
6. Your selling price if a retail item, or percentage of gross price of completed product, if used for manufacturing or service
7. The date you place an order
8. The number of items and the date they are received

Then, every time you sell or use an item, write it down and subtract it from the last balance. You should also indicate the reorder number, based on when and by how much you must replenish your stock.

The reorder number will be determined by such factors as the following:

1. The minimum cost per unit available from your supplier, including quantity discounts, preseason specials, and discounts for cash or quick payment
2. The delivery schedule—the delay between placing the order and receiving it
3. Economic and social trends that can affect the way an item is perceived by the public

For example, during a depressed or inflated economy, sales for leisure or discretionary items typically drop. By keeping an eye on

these factors, you can adjust your inventory needs accordingly and not get stuck with great quantities of items that you can't move.

After a while, you will be able to recognize at a glance which items are movers and which are simply taking up shelf space. When you reach this point, your ordering skills will become much more efficient and your investment in inventory will become a profitable proposition.

Notes

Key Points

Personal Thoughts

Additional Research

18

MAKING THE MOST
OF YOUR TIME

A recent survey of small business owners indicated that one of the qualities they felt contributed the most to their success was organization. In conjunction with this is the fact that time management and basic organizational seminars continue to be the most popular offerings in adult education catalogs and business workshops around the country.

Time is money! It is vital to your success that you learn to manage your time and organize paperwork. This might sound rather simplistic, but you would be amazed at the number of small business owners who operate in a constant state of chaos.

Although we have seen a number of "A messy office is the sign of a creative mind" posters on entrepreneurs' office walls, it is a good bet that the holders of these signs can recount story after story of missing checks, lost orders, or misplaced files, which disrupted or halted the flow of business until they were located.

The survey respondents also stated that once they had learned to manage their time in both their personal and business lives and had set up guidelines for handling routine tasks,

they felt more confident about accepting new challenges and making decisions.

The simple truth about getting organized is that it clears your mind for taking care of the nitty-gritty, profit-making aspects of being in business—production and promotion. For example, just by setting aside a certain place in your work area to hold customer files and billing information, you have made one major step toward maximizing production. Knowing that all the supplies and materials needed to conduct your business are located in one place saves you both time and energy.

Making Time Work for You

Time management is the ability to take the hours we have available and use them to our advantage. Making lists of tasks to be done and giving them a priority rating is one of the best ways to avoid losing precious moments.

Keep a monthly calendar handy to help you keep track of major commitments, important dates, and appointments. Try to avoid using it for notations of daily work in progress, carryover tasks, or other things that are best suited for inclusion on your daily and weekly lists. There are several other ideas you can easily incorporate into your working lifestyle that will maximize your productivity.

Work Smart

Handle the jobs you find most difficult or cumbersome during peak performance time. If you are a morning person and find that making telephone calls to potential customers is one of your least favorite tasks, make those calls first thing in the morning when you are feeling fresh and energetic. Then organize the rest of the day's tasks accordingly.

Set Realistic Daily Goals for Yourself

Just because you are the key employee, don't try to do everything at once. Learn just how much work you can accept and expect to accomplish in a given period of time and allow yourself to turn down work if it seems like it will be too much for you to handle.

Positive Reinforcement

When you work alone, as many small business owners do when getting their businesses off the ground, there generally aren't many people around to support or praise your work...and everyone needs strokes! Remember that a customer's praises are proof that you are doing a good job.

Reward Yourself

Sometimes it is easy to forget that you are important to the business—you *are* the business. So treat yourself to a special dinner now and then or plan an evening where you go out to a movie or do something else that has absolutely nothing to do with business. Remind yourself that this is your reward for accomplishing certain goals for your business. It will help to keep your spirits high.

Don't Procrastinate

Don't put off doing tasks that must be done. If you constantly let some tasks slide because you don't enjoy doing them or they are boring and time-consuming, you will soon find yourself back-logged and unable to catch up. The effects of procrastination may not be obvious until you are faced with a deadline and, at that point, you will realize that you are working at less than maximum efficiency using the wrong supplies, feeling tense, and being hassled by minor problems that could have been avoided. Even when business is slow and it seems that there could be little harm done by taking a day off to go to the beach, be sure to complete all your required tasks before closing up shop.

Limit Personal Phone Calls

Ask friends and relatives not to call during established business hours. These friendly calls not only eat into productive time, they tie up the line when an important client may be trying to get in touch with you. The same holds true with visitors. If you are self-employed, friends and family often feel that you are not really "working" and that they can stop by anytime to chat. Explain that you will be happy to visit with them at some other time and be sure to tell them why so there aren't any ill feelings.

Obviously, there will be times when unavoidable situations arise, such as an emergency or an unexpected problem. Take these into consideration by estimating how long a project will take and then adding a bit of extra time to give yourself some leeway.

Delegate

If you find that you absolutely cannot handle a certain aspect of the business, such as your own bookkeeping, for example, don't labor over the task—you will end up wasting a great deal of time and could make some serious mistakes. Admit to yourself that the task is just not your strong point and make arrangements to have someone else do it.

Learn to Say "No"

One of the hardest things for most people to do is to say "no." Even when we realize that helping a friend out on a special project will cost valuable time, we often agree to do it because we hate to say no. What we do is justify our acceptance by assuring ourselves that saying yes will put us in the position of meeting a lot of potential customers. The reality is that using that time to make phone calls or a sales call for your own business will probably result in a paying customer, not just a potential contact.

Minimize Business Meetings

Before setting up a formal meeting, which can be very time-consuming, see if you can take care of the matter by phone or through the mail. If a meeting can't be avoided, make sure you specify a time limit to encourage people to get down to business. Another time-saving device for meetings is to work up an agenda that outlines exactly what has to be discussed to avoid idle chit-chat and unnecessary diversions.

Plan Your Time

When you have to run errands, plan them for a sensible time, such as in the morning when traffic is light. Plan to do as many things as possible in one trip, outlining the stops you must make so they follow a sequential order.

Notes

Key Points

Personal Thoughts

Additional Research

19

MANAGING THE BUSINESS

Doing the Work

You've chosen your service, you've taken care of equipment needs, you've done some advertising and promotion. Now what? No one is beating down your doors for business! What should you do?

Relax. You're going to discover that few catering services— few small businesses at all, for that matter— get off the ground like a rocket. There's only one reason you should panic if you don't get a great deal of business right away, and that's if you've made this new catering venture your sole source of projected income. There's a simple way to avoid that problem:

Don't make catering your primary source of income—at least not at first.

Unless you are independently wealthy and can cover yourself financially, you should not try to start in this business full-time. There are simply too many variables that you can't control.

Build the Business Slowly

Although there are people who have jumped into the business with both feet, nearly everyone with whom we spoke claims it is better

to start part-time, a few jobs here and there, and work your way into the business. This not only will help you ease your way into the job, it also will help you maintain interest and momentum since you won't be facing any expectations of immediate success.

The best advice we can offer on starting your business and maintaining momentum is

1. Start slow

2. Go slow

3. Grow slow

4. Learn fast

Keep in mind as you move along with your new business that the catering business is specialized, and there are specific knowledge and skills you must have to stay competitive.

There are numerous sources through which you can gain this knowledge. Books are invaluable, and there are any number to choose from. Trade publications are another valuable resource. (See the Appendix.)

> *It is not enough to have great qualities, we should also have management of them.*
> La Rochefoucauld

Professional seminars, cooking classes, and adult education classes all are ways to build on your skills and keep up with your competitors. One of the most overlooked sources of knowledge for professional growth is your clientele. *Listen* to them when they give you feedback about the service you provide.

Managing the Business

Up until now, you've been given information on basic planning for your business's start-up. Now it's time to look at some specifics of running your catering operation on a day-to-day basis.

One of the first things you must consistently do is find out what your prospective clients want. To hit the market with a product or service without first gauging how it will be received is silly at best and, at worst, it can be financially disastrous.

Another aspect of managing the business is your contract, as described in Chapter 16. This is important both for your business records and as a document that protects both you and the customer. The best method of protection in all eventualities is to develop a standard contract that clearly spells out the services you will provide, as well as specific requests and payment policies. It might be worth the expense to print these forms on NCR (noncarbon reproducing) paper, so you can keep a copy for your records. Talk with an attorney prior to finalizing any customer contracts, just to make sure you've covered all your bases.

Responsible Conduct

Legalities and contracts are just one aspect of an important part of business management. Know your responsibilities and those of your client, and make sure he or she knows as well. Each of you has certain expectations of the other that contracts cannot cover.
You are responsible to your client for:

1. *Quality.* You must deliver the best service and product you can. For a catering service, people expect great food that is attractively presented.

2. *Timeliness.* In catering, it is essential that services be provided on time.

3. *Fair pricing.* Depending on the group and the food, prices will vary by job, but you should always charge what is reasonable. If you charge too much, your reputation—and opportunity for future prospects—will suffer.

4. *Willingness to correct mistakes.* Learn to recognize when an error is yours or the client's. If you are at fault, take immediate steps to correct the problem, because you want that customer's business again. If the customer is at fault, show support in helping to correct the problem.

5. *Full attention.* Clients appreciate a service that considers their work to be privileged and treats it as such.

6. *Friendly attitude.* A smile and a genuine concern about the client and his or her occasion is important.

The customer's responsibilities to you are to:

1. Be clear when giving you a job
2. Keep the job within the scope of agreed-upon services
3. Pay promptly for your work, or as agreed upon
4. Give you the opportunity to correct mistakes

Making sure the unwritten expectations are clear from the outset of any business transaction will not only prevent problems, it will also make you a more efficient business owner.

Remember that problems will occur. The catering business is not immune to Murphy's Law. (If you're not familiar with Murphy's Law, it says, in essence, "If anything can go wrong, it will.")

Being Prepared

You need to be aware of things that *can* go wrong, so when they *do* go wrong, you have at least some idea of what your options are. To protect yourself from the worst twists of Murphy's Law, plan on covering yourself with:

1. Enough food
2. Enough staff

Why should you buy a little extra food? Because you never know if the client's state-of-the-art oven is going to char your first batch of stuffed mushrooms after only 10 minutes. Or if the 30 guests have magically become 35.

It is important to have enough staff to troubleshoot any last minute problems that occur. Because catering demands that a lot of action takes place in a short window of time, it is essential that you not scrimp on personpower.

Establishing Hours

In this business you have flexibility in establishing your office hours, but little say in when you actually cater an occasion. You will need to reserve some hours each day to take care of office work and to be available to new and prospective clients. However,

the hours that you work will be largely dictated by whether or not you have a catering job on that day.

Notes

Key Points

Personal Thoughts

Additional Research

20

HIRING EMPLOYEES

Your Catering Staff

Because the nature of the catering business requires that many tasks be done at approximately the same time, it is not possible for a caterer to handle most jobs alone. Many caterers recruit a few friends or family members to help with the first few jobs, but soon realize the necessity for hired help.

> *Knowledge is of two kinds. We know a subject ourselves or we know where we can find information on it.*
>
> Samuel Johnson

Part-time employees who will work as independent contractors on an as-needed basis are ideal for catering. The size and occasion of the catered event dictate the number of cooks and servers needed.

Catering companies require chefs, assistant cooks, prep cooks, wait staff, clean-up crew, dishwashers, and bartenders. More often than not, members of the catering team will fill more than one of these positions during a single event. For example, once the cooking is finished,

an assistant cook can play the role of waitperson and then dish-washer.

Depending on the function, it may be necessary to hire a host to seat guests and a head waiter to coordinate the efforts of the serving staff. As the business grows, many of the responsibilities of the caterer can be turned over to a project or banquet manager who will oversee the entire planning and execution of functions.

According to the National Association of Catering Executives, three servers are required for every twenty-five guests at a formal sit-down dinner, two servers per twenty-five guests at a buffet, and one server for every twenty-five attendees at a cocktail reception. Figure on hiring one bartender for every fifty guests. Generally, one chef can handle meals for up to one hundred guests, with support from an assistant cook and one or two prep cooks.

It is in your best interest not to scrimp on personnel for a job; it is better to have a couple of extra bodies available than to have too few people trying to do too much. The latter situation will frustrate your employees and possibly disappoint your client and the guests.

Finding Qualified Staff

You can find employees by running ads in the classified section of your local paper and by listing the job at college and university student-employment offices (many schools offer Food and Beverage Management courses—a perfect resource of students for your part-time needs). Also ask friends, relatives, and restaurant employees in your area for referrals.

Ask applicants to complete a standard employment application (available in any stationery store) and to provide references from former employers. Check these references carefully to ascertain that applicants are responsible, honest, and hard-working. Schedule a personal interview with each applicant to make your own determination about personality, level of interest in the job, abilities, and future goals. Explain that the work may be sporadic; if this does not deter the applicant, add his or her name to your roster of potential employees.

Another option is to register with a temporary help agency. The agency will screen and interview applicants and will then

recommend the most qualified people. Agencies will charge you an hourly fee for each employee you hire for a job.

There are advantages and disadvantages to both options. Hiring employees yourself is less expensive than going through an agency, but it is also more time-consuming. By hiring employees yourself, you can assess each one's suitability to a specific job, and over time will learn what to expect from each of them. Further, you will have the opportunity to train employees who work for you on a regular basis. On the other hand, because you are *their* client, reputable temporary agencies will expend considerable time and energy to find you reliable employees.

Pay Scales

Service personnel are generally paid between $4.50 and $6.00 per hour and are given a 15 percent gratuity per job. Rates for good cooks are high; rates for great cooks can range into the hundreds of dollars for one night's work. Kitchen helpers start at minimum wage.

When it comes time to hire a project manager, plan to spend between $10.00 and $20.00 per hour for their services. Bartenders typically earn $10.00 to $25.00 per hour depending on the region.

On-the-Job Training

When you find someone who seems to have all the qualifications needed, arrange to train him or her on the job. Many owners like to do this themselves, to ensure that their standards are instilled from the beginning and to get a first-hand idea of the new recruit's work habits. If you have a trusted employee, have the new recruit accompany your staffer on assignments to learn the ropes. (This extra duty should always result in a bonus for the employee doing the training.)

Training may take several days or weeks, depending on the worker's previous experience. Basically, a good training process should involve the following steps:

1. Gain the recruit's confidence by putting him or her at ease.
2. Find out what he or she already knows.

3. Indicate the importance of the specific task being taught.

4. Explain and demonstrate each step patiently.

5. Be sure each step is understood before moving on to the next.

6. Encourage and welcome questions.

7. Have the recruit try to do the task.

8. Correct mistakes gently.

9. Have him or her repeat the steps for you.

10. When you are both comfortable, let the recruit go out on his or her own.

11. Review performance periodically.

12. Offer support by letting the employee train others when ready.

Taking time to train properly reduces turnover and accidents, improves the quality of work performed, lowers your cost of labor, and increases productivity. Every time you have to replace an employee and train a new one, you're losing productivity.

Overtraining the Ambitious

Sometimes it is possible to train people so well they feel they can start their own business in competition with yours. This can occur when an employee realizes you are making money off his or her hard work. There are several ways to stay on top of your employees' activities.

If you're sure an employee is thinking of starting a business, take him or her aside and explain the administrative aspects of the business. Find out if he or she truly realizes that you are providing steady work on a regular basis and if it's really clear how much is involved in running a business.

In rare cases, you are going to lose an employee who feels confident enough to start a business, and there isn't too much you can do about it.

In other situations, you can promote the employee by making him or her a senior executive or sales manager, as appropriate.

This is feasible only if your cash flow and the employee's ability warrant it.

The Benefits of Happy Employees

Personnel management is a time-consuming job for the business owner. However, paying attention to the needs of your employees and working to gain their trust and maintain their loyalty can do nothing but benefit your business.

The attitude of your employees about your management techniques plays an important part in building and maintaining your reputation in the business world. If employees are treated fairly and with respect, their job satisfaction will be reflected in the way they do their jobs.

This is something that can truly keep you ahead of the competition; a loyal, efficient, and enthusiastic group of workers is one of your most effective forms of public relations, so never scrimp when it comes to keeping your employees happy. A few important rules of thumb in dealing with employees include the following:

♦ *Never expect an employee to do something you wouldn't do.* This is why training new recruits yourself is such a good idea; it shows them that you are willing and able to step in and do anything that needs to be done.

♦ *Listen to your employees.* Talk to your staff regularly and incorporate any ideas they have whenever feasible. Remember that they have firsthand knowledge about how certain aspects of the job are done and might know if they can be done more efficiently. Suggestions that work for the good of the company should be rewarded with a bonus.

♦ *Take the time to talk about business standards and practices.* Make sure everyone knows exactly what is expected of them. Outline duties and responsibilities on the job and schedule regular reviews to ensure that they are constantly met. If you find it necessary to talk to an employee about work habits, do it in private. And do not

criticize; offer constructive ways that performance can be improved.

◆ *Treat each employee as an individual.* When someone seems to be having personal problems that are interfering with his or her work, be willing to allow him or her time off without penalty to take care of the situation. An employee plagued with problems may carry them to work, and this could have a negative effect on productivity. It is much better to get someone to fill in until the regular employee is operating at full efficiency again.

Representing Your Business

As representatives of your business, your employees should be polite, neat, and efficient. Uniforms, which you will supply, should always be clean and ironed; fingernails should be clean and manicured; and hair should be kept neat and trimmed (kitchen workers should wear a cap or net).

Your reputation depends on the professionalism and demeanor of those working for you, so be sure they are the kind of people you would want to serve you at your own party.

Sanitation and Safety Standards

The Board of Health will demand that you institute a strict sanitation program to protect food against contamination and to maintain a high standard of cleanliness. It is also important to establish a comprehensive safety program to prevent accidents.

Everyone working in your kitchen must be aware of the importance of obeying sanitation and safety rules, which will be supplied to you by the Board of Health on approval of the workspace.

Most of the rules that you will be expected to follow seem obvious, but health inspectors continually find violations during their unannounced visits to facilities. One state inspector estimates that 85 percent of his visits to restaurant and catering kitchens result in a warning or a citation.

Post a list of guidelines in a central location and review it periodically with all employees. Make it a policy to give a warning

the first time someone violates sanitation or safety rules, and to dismiss the employee if he or she is responsible for another violation.

Sanitation Rules

1. All workers must wear clean aprons or uniforms in the kitchen.

2. Kitchen workers must cover their hair with a hat or hairnet.

3. Employees must wash their hands (including fingernails) with soap and warm water before starting work, after using the restroom, and when beginning preparation of a menu item.

4. Soap and paper towels must be available in the kitchen and restrooms.

5. Smoking is prohibited at all times in the kitchen area.

6. Restroom and kitchen surfaces, including floors, sinks, fixtures, and waste receptacles must be cleaned daily with hot, soapy water or disinfectant cleanser.

7. Food waste must be placed into a garbage disposal or stored in airtight, leak-proof containers that are regularly removed.

8. Garbage containers must be cleaned and disinfected after being emptied.

9. Food must be prepared only in areas specifically designated for food preparation.

10. Dishes, utensils, and cookware must be sanitized or sterilized immediately after use and put away as soon as possible. Glassware should be washed and sterilized separately in fresh, hot water.

11. Perishable food products must be refrigerated as soon as received and checked against the purchase order while the deliveryperson is present.

12. During transport to the catering location, food—cooked or uncooked—must be carefully and securely packed in containers to keep it fresh and clean.

Safety Rules

1. Keep sharp instruments in their proper place.
2. Keep floors clean, dry, and free of clutter for safe access at all times.
3. Use potholders or oven mitts when handling hot pots or pans.
4. Limit the use of glass in the kitchen as much as possible.
5. Keep drawers and cupboard doors closed.
6. Wear proper work shoes and uniforms or aprons.
7. Treat cuts and wounds immediately and sterilize knives, chopping boards, and other equipment being used. If the cut is on the hand, wear rubber gloves while working with food until the wound heals.
8. Keep electrical equipment— especially slicers, electric knives, and mixers—turned off and covered when not in use.
9. Make sure work areas are well lighted and ventilated.
10. Keep a first-aid kit fully stocked and easily accessible.
11. Make two trips rather than carry too much at one time.
12. Use a dolly or get assistance when lifting or moving heavy items.

Notes

Key Points

Personal Thoughts

Additional Research

21

ADVERTISING YOUR BUSINESS

More than 150 years ago, Thomas Macaulay, a British historian and statesman, said, "Advertising is to business what steam is to industry. [They provide] the same propelling power."

Few in business would argue with Macaulay's observation—it is as true today as it was when steam was the driving force behind industry. But the question remains, "How do you get the most out of your advertising dollar?" The answer is to

1. Know your customer

2. Target your market

3. Understand the basics of advertising

In this chapter, we will provide an overview of various aspects of advertising, including how to use circulation figures to figure your cost per thousand (CPM) and how to create ads that will bring results.

What Is Advertising?

Advertising informs the public about:

♦ Who you are

- ◆ What kind of business you operate
- ◆ How they can buy your products or services
- ◆ Why they should come to you

Before you even open the doors of your business, you should start thinking about your advertising program—how much money you can afford to spend, where your dollars will be best spent, and how to structure your campaign.

Decide what kind of results you want. Are you looking for immediate sales or ongoing recognition? What kind of customers are you hoping to attract? Are you emphasizing price, service, workmanship, or something unique? Once you have answered these questions, your decision as to the best type of advertising for the allotted dollars will be easier to make.

There are three basic types of advertising that you will be most interested in during the first few years of your business.

Start-up Advertising

This includes your business cards and stationery, announcement flyers and brochures, and your initial ads in newspapers or other publications. At this point, your main focus will be on telling people where you are located and what you can offer them.

Ongoing Advertising

Once the business is up and running, it will be vital to your success to institute a regular advertising campaign that is well thought out and—this is the key—consistent. Your goal at this point is to attract new clients, obtain repeat business from existing clients, and enhance your reputation.

Appearance Advertising

After you have reached the point where your business is on steady ground and you're showing increased profits every year, you can afford to dabble in "institutional advertising," as it is called in the trade. This is where you pick up the tab to send a dozen kids to the rodeo when it comes to town, or you sponsor a float in the local

parade and, in return, get your name listed on the program or on a banner in the parade. This is primarily name recognition only and, while every little bit is helpful, by the time you can afford it, you probably will be in pretty good shape anyway.

Advertising Your Catering Business

It isn't necessary to spend great amounts of money to advertise your catering service. You will soon find that much of your business is the result of word-of-mouth advertising—someone attending a function you catered calls because of the high-quality service and the wonderful food you provided. You cater his or her party, which results in calls from his or her guests, and so on.

Some very successful caterers claim that they rarely, if ever, advertise but merely hand out business cards. The best bet, however, is to develop a low-cost, ongoing campaign, especially when the business is just getting started, to get and keep your name in the public consciousness. This will guarantee that the business will grow consistently.

If you are located in a community of under 500,000, advertising in local newspapers is a cost-effective way to go. A consistently run classified ad will be more effective in the long run than a display ad that you may only be able to run on occasion.

But don't dismiss the possibility of running small display ads on a seasonal basis, focusing on promoting your services for graduations and weddings in May and June or office and private parties during the winter holiday season.

Consider offering an incentive, such as a 10 percent discount on parties of over fifty guests, free coffee service for afternoon teas, or something equally attractive to people who mention seeing the ad. This will give you an opportunity to test the response rate at certain times of the year and help you in planning future advertising campaigns.

Classified Ads

Don't underestimate the power of classified ads. Many major corporations utilize the classifieds even though they have sizable

budgets available for display advertising. There are several reasons for this.

1. The classifieds are an extremely reliable testing ground for new products, services, and ideas. Although it's true that people who typically read the classifieds are different from those who scan display ads, they are considered to be responsive and, therefore, can give you a very good idea of whether or not you have placed your ad in the appropriate publication.

2. A short, well-written classified in the right publication and under the proper category can be a low-cost method of advertising that guarantees solid returns.

3. If a company is trying to establish a mailing list, a classified ad that features an "Inquiry" statement, such as "Send name and address for free details (or a brochure)," is a good way to build up a file of potential customers' names. By spending the time, energy, and postage to get the information, these respondents have expressed interest in your business and can be considered good prospects.

4. Classified ads are inexpensive, ranging from 50¢ to $15 per word, depending on the publication. With careful planning, you should be able to get broad-based coverage without putting a dent in your operating capital.

Here's an example:

June Brides and Graduates

Plan now for the celebration of this important milestone. *YOUR CATERING COMPANY* will help make it special by offering a unique menu and personalized service at a reasonable price. Call 555-5555 today for a free consultation.

Display Advertising

Don't dismiss the possibility of running small display ads on a seasonal basis, even though they are more expensive than classified advertising. Focus on promoting through display advertising during specific times of the year when you know that certain markets will need your services.

Choose your publications wisely, concentrating on related trade publications. Consider offering an incentive, such as a 10 percent discount if customers bring in the ad. This will help you track responses and plan future display ad campaigns.

As with all types of advertising, it is important to define your market when getting ready to place a display ad. Your main goal should be to select a publication that will reach the audience you want and then create a specific ad that appeals to that target group.

To Write or Not to Write?

Writing display ad copy is not for the inexperienced. Although it is possible to learn how to put ideas and words together that will get the results you desire, it is recommended that you hire a copywriter if you have any qualms about producing an ad.

However, if you are confident that you can develop your own ad, remember that it must build identity through the use of carefully planned words and design. Glance through newspapers and magazines to find ads that catch your eye. Most likely, the ones that stand out have a memorable logo, effective use of space, or an unusual headline that leads you into the body of the ad. These are ads you should refer to as samples when designing your own.

When planning your ad, keep the following elements in mind:

1. *Visibility.* Your ad may be surrounded by many others, so design it so that it will immediately attract the reader's attention.

2. *Boldness.* Use large art and/or a bold headline as a focal point.

3. **Simplicity.** Don't overwhelm the reader with too many fine details. The ad's main point is lost and so is the reader's attention. This is particularly true in a small ad.

4. **White space.** Just because you have, say, a four-by-six-inch space to work with, it isn't necessary to fill it up. In fact, white space is a necessary component in assuring your ad will be read.

5. **Use simple-to-read typefaces.** The easiest fonts to read are *serif* typefaces, such as Times Roman and Bookman, that have tiny lines at the tops and bottoms of the letters. *Sans serif* (without strokes) typefaces, such as Helvetica, are fine for ads containing only a few words, but are difficult for the eye to follow when there is a lot of text. Also, be sure that the type is large enough; generally nothing smaller than 10-point type should be used. If type is too small to read, it will simply be ignored.

Design and Typesetting

It isn't necessary to be a great artist to create an ad, especially these days with the availability of a variety of impressive graphic software programs. In addition, you can buy cut-out-and-transfer (press-on) letters in different typefaces, symbols, borders, and designs through graphic-art-supply companies. Most word processing programs also contain computer graphics that can dress up your ad at a low cost.

If you feel uncomfortable about laying out your ad so it has eye appeal, consider hiring an art student to handle the job for a prearranged fee or as a school assignment. (Talk with the head of the art department to see if there is a work/study for credit program.) Just be sure to review the student's work prior to making a commitment.

Also, check with the advertising department of the newspaper or magazine you are planning to advertise in. There may be graphic artists or designers on staff who will work on the layout for you. In fact, there are still newspapers in the country that offer full service, from ad concept to design work, at a minimal charge to their advertising clients.

Publications work on tight deadlines so be sure you start the process early enough to get a proof copy of your ad back in time to make any corrections. You can imagine the anguish of seeing your ad appear with the wrong address. Although the publication would probably do a "make-good" for you and run a corrected ad at no charge, the damage has already been done. The final responsibility for the ad rests on you, so, as with any other aspect of your business, plan ahead.

Sample Display Advertisement:

Formal Dinner for 10?
Buffet Luncheon for 100?
Outdoor Picnic for 1,000?

Discover
YOUR CATERING COMPANY

We handle all the details
and leave the fun for you!

Call us today for a free consultation.
Mention this ad and get a 10% discount.

YOUR CATERING COMPANY
555-5555

Yellow Pages

In cities of more than 50,000, your Yellow Page advertising is crucial to success. But don't settle for a tiny listing under "Caterers," as it is likely the reader will gloss over it. Ask the Yellow Page representative for details on buying a display ad that will help your business stand out from the rest. Few successful businesspersons claim to build their businesses strictly by word-of-mouth referrals. If you're planning to structure a full-scale operation, placing a listing in the Yellow Pages is an absolute necessity.

> *Advertising is the greatest art form of the 20th Century.*
> Marshall McLuhan

Listing in the Yellow Pages requires installation of a business telephone, even if you are starting the business from your home. A potential client will think it unprofessional to have his or her call answered by a child or by someone answering with a simple "Hello."

Check with the Yellow Page Directory advertising representative to find out when the directory in your area is published. Because directories come out at different times of year depending on the region, it may be necessary to develop a supplemental newspaper advertising or other promotional campaign.

If, for example, you plan to open for business in August and the phone book in your area comes out in March of next year, you do not want to lose eight months of valuable exposure to prospective clients by doing no promotion during that time.

Specialty Items

Specialty advertising refers to matches, pens, key chains and similar items that have a company's name printed on them. The theory behind this type of advertising is that every time you use the item, you think about the firm.

Investigate the items you can have printed by visiting a specialty advertising representative (listed in the Yellow Pages under "Advertising"). Notepads, pens, pencils, and desk calendars are among your best forms of specialty advertising. Consider items

that relate specifically to your business—measuring cups, mugs, wine glasses, napkins, aprons, etc.

Direct Mail

Another way to target specific markets is through direct mail using brochures, flyers, and other materials outlining your catering business and detailing the benefits of your service. Recent postal increases have made direct mail a more expensive proposition than it used to be, but if you mail only to select groups or zip codes, it can be worthwhile.

Mailing lists, broken down by zip codes, income brackets and other specific factors, can be purchased inexpensively from some printers, advertising agencies, local publications, and mailing list brokers. Check in the library for a *Direct Mail List Rate and Data* volume to find brokers in the areas you desire.

If you do institute a direct mail program, be sure to send regular announcements to those who have responded to ads in the past but didn't buy your goods or use your service.

Circumstances frequently change, and sending reminders that you are still in business offering quality service at a fair price is sure to result in response at some point.

Be aware that the average return for direct mail is between 1 percent and 2.5 percent. Therefore, don't expect the phone to ring off the hook every time you send a mailing; consistency is the important factor here.

Tracking Advertisement Response

Some customers will tell you that they saw your ad and might even let you know what they liked or disliked about it if you ask them. Even so, you should develop other methods for determining if your advertising is working.

One simple method is to include a coupon in the ad and then to count the number of coupons redeemed within a certain period of time. However, because even the most well-intentioned people often cut coupons, file them, and totally forget about them, this method is not foolproof.

Sample Flyer

YOUR CATERING COMPANY

Your Event Is Our Top Priority

We Happily Take Care of Every Detail
to Make Your Occasion a Special One.

**WEDDINGS
ANNIVERSARIES
BIRTHDAYS
GRADUATIONS
OPEN HOUSES
BUSINESS MEETINGS
FUNDRAISERS
INTIMATE DINNERS
GROUP PICNICS**

...and just about any
CELEBRATION
you can think of!

Call for a Free Consultation

555-5555

Sample Direct Mail Letter

YOUR CATERING COMPANY

1 Main Street 555-5555

Mr. Robert Director
Large Corporation
Central Avenue
Anytown, USA

Dear Mr. Director,

Your annual Christmas Party and Benefit Dinner was highly publicized in the *Daily Tribune* this year. Congratulations on raising $1,500 for the Children's Foundation in town. It is the efforts of corporations like yours that make the difference to these wonderful organizations.

Since you host a number of functions throughout the year, from employee get-togethers to stockholder meetings, I would like to offer the services of *YOUR CATERING COMPANY* for your next function.

We offer customized menus designed with your needs in mind, including hot and cold foods to suit any occasion, from sit-down dinners to management meeting buffets. Our staff is a highly trained, reliable group of professionals who have served a wide variety of guests, from politicians to new business owners. They respect protocol and maintain integrity in their work.

I will call next week to see if we can arrange a meeting to discuss your needs and our ability to fill them. I will be happy to provide the names of other companies we have served in this capacity.

Yours very truly,
Katie Smith
Your Catering Company

So, although you will be able to gauge response to some degree, be aware that many of the people who come into or call your business have probably seen the coupon but simply mislaid or forgotten it.

Predicting Ad Response

There is a standardized formula in advertising that provides a barometer for predicting how much response can be expected from either a display or classified ad. The formula states that you will see one-half of the total responses from an ad within a certain period of time after receiving your first inquiry or order.

For an ad run in a daily newspaper, the period of time is three days; for a weekly newspaper or magazine, it is six days; within fifteen days for a monthly publication; and within twenty-five days when running in a bimonthly. Although there will be exceptions to this rule, it does give you a base from which to track response.

Determining Your Cost Per Thousand

The cost per thousand (CPM) equation can help you develop a cost-effective campaign by telling you what the ad cost per thousand readers will be. Most publications will provide a CPM comparison on request (some include it in their media kits), but you can easily figure it out for yourself with just a few facts from the publications you approach.

For convenience sake, CPM equations are typically based on the rate of a full-page black-and-white ad. You simply divide the full-page rate by the thousands of circulation. It is important that you get the circulation, *not* the readership, because magazines and newspapers typically claim that their readership is 2 to 50 percent higher because of "pass-along" of the publication to friends or relatives.

For example, if a certain newspaper is charging $2,000 for a full-page ad, and it claims the true circulation is 200,000, you will be paying $10 per 1,000 readers for your ad space. Another specialized publication's full-page rate may be $1,000 with a circulation of 50,000. The cost per 1,000 readers will be much higher—$20 per 1,000—but the cost may be justified if your product or service is especially suited to this market.

Benefits of Paid Circulation

It is also important to know that publications with a paid circulation generally have a readership that is more inclined to respond to advertising. This is because of the simple fact that they are a captive audience who have taken the time to *order* the publication. This is especially valuable if you have a product or service that you're planning to market through mail-order channels.

You can find circulation, readership demographics, advertising rates, and other important information about a number of publications (especially those with national distribution) through *Standard Rate and Data Service (SRDS)*, available through the research desk of your local library.

The Advertising Research Foundation and the Association of Business Publishers conducted a study to determine the impact of advertising on the sale of products. Several different products were used for the study, and each was advertised for a twelve-month period in an appropriate publication. The results were interesting but not surprising to anyone who has ever utilized a solid advertising campaign in promoting a business.

♦ More advertising meant more sales.

♦ Determining results from an ad campaign generally took four to six months. One or two insertions did not indicate viable results.

♦ Color in advertisements dramatically increased response and sales.

♦ A well-developed ad campaign keeps on working for a year and sometimes even longer in publications with high "keep" appeal.

Knowledge and confidence in your service, faith in yourself, and respect for your customers are the keys to successfully building your future. As you go about starting and establishing your business, remember the word "profit." This alone should give you the necessary motivation to get out there and confidently tell the world what you have to offer.

Notes

Key Points

Personal Thoughts

Additional Research

22

PROMOTION AND PUBLIC RELATIONS

Informing the public about your business through the use of business cards, brochures, mailing pieces, catalogs, and specialty items (calendars, pens, and T-shirts imprinted with your company name) is a form of advertising that is known as promotion; what you do over and above your paid advertising and promotion that help build your image and keep your business in the public consciousness are referred to as public relations. There is a fine line between the two, and they can make or break your business if not addressed.

There are many clever ways to extend the effectiveness of your advertising and promotional dollars, as illustrated in the following examples.

A Little Creativity Goes a Long Way

The owner of a pet grooming business leaves a business card and a brochure featuring a 20 percent discount coupon everywhere he goes. When he is running errands, he always takes a handful of

brochures with him to hand to store clerks, gas station attendants, and even foodservers he runs into during the day.

If he sees a car with a dog in it, or one with a bumper sticker announcing the owner's affection for a pet, he slips a brochure under the windshield wiper. Does it work? Absolutely. He claims that 45 percent of his new business comes from the recipients of his handouts, and the majority of them become regular customers.

Another business owner who operates a small walking tour service in her beachside town sends out a one-page quarterly newsletter featuring historical and other facts about the area to everyone who has ever taken the tour. She includes a $10 coupon that can be redeemed by former clients or their guests.

> *Advertisements contain the only truths to be relied on in a newspaper.*
>
> Thomas Jefferson

She states that many of her clients are local residents who send their out-of-town visitors on her walking tour, simply because she makes sure they are aware that she is still in business and generates enthusiasm through the newsletter.

Charity Tie-ins

Other ideas you might consider include promoting humanitarian outreach. For example, for every ten products a customer buys or every tenth time a customer uses your service, you donate a predetermined amount of money to a local charity. You can easily keep track of customers' purchases by punching a hole at the edge of a card designed by you or your printer strictly for that purpose.

When you are ready to present the check to the particular charity, make sure the chairperson of the organization is there to accept it and be sure to contact the local press and invite them to the "event." In most cases, you'll receive free coverage.

According to successful entrepreneurs, free giveaways are the most successful promotions. You can order items such as pens, pencils, notepads, and calendars, just to name a few, with your name and phone number printed on them to give to people. Every time the recipient uses the item, he or she will automatically think

of you! Check under "Advertising Specialties" in the Yellow Pages for prices and ideas.

You might want to consider giving away catering services through a contest or drawing. Likewise, you might also think about participating in activities held at church or school bazaars, civic meetings, business organization events, or fraternal club events (Elks, Moose, Rotarians, etc.). Pay attention to how other catering businesses promote with giveaways and see how much business it brings in. All it costs you is a little time and not much money.

Reminder Cards

Sending regular "thinking-of-you" cards to your past and present clientele is especially effective with service businesses. Again, it assures the customer that you are friendly, reliable, and conscientious—real pluses for your credibility.

Networking

Check out local business-owner groups and the chamber of commerce in your area. Pay your membership dues and join as many groups as possible. Membership in these organizations offers you the opportunity to meet people who might use your service and will, at bare minimum, tell others about you once they know you, feel comfortable with you, and understand what you are offering. You will also be given a listing in the group's directory, generally under your specific category.

And, as is so often the case, members are prone to supporting others involved with their group. It is quite possible that members with compatible businesses (such as florists, photographers, bridal shops, bakeries, and party shops) will put a stack of your cards or brochures on their counter or in their referral file. In return, you may be able to promote their businesses to your customers. This is the true meaning of networking.

The directory also gives you bona-fide access to an instant mailing list, which you can use to send out promotional flyers or brochures. Your participation in the organization's events and the willingness, for example, to speak at functions about your area of specialization will let people know that you are community-minded.

This involvement will work to project a positive image for you and your business.

Customer Service

One of the most overlooked areas in promoting business is the way we create an impression when dealing with the public on a one-to-one basis. The ageless philosophy that the customer is always right and comes first has, it seems, gotten lost in the shuffle in these days of fast-paced transactions.

As a small business owner, you can be sure that customers will flock to you if you make them feel important. It is as easy as greeting them warmly (instruct your employees, if you have them, to do the same), maintaining a courteous attitude, and inviting them to come back soon- even if they have not spent any money.

Remember that word travels fast, and if you create an atmosphere that makes all your customers feel special, you can be sure they will tell their friends and neighbors.

Free Publicity

Free publicity also comes under the category of public relations. This includes newspaper, magazine, radio, and television interviews that feature interesting or unusual facts about you and your business.

As any newspaper reporter or talk-show host will tell you, everybody has a story to tell. The key is to get the media to zero in on yours and make it available to the public. If you have trouble deciding on a unique angle for your story, invite several friends over for a brainstorming session to create a newsworthy item.

Use your imagination to explore the creative possibilities of your business venture. And then look at your personal story. Perhaps you have completely switched fields with your new business: There's a story with a strong slant toward risk-taking. Maybe you have successfully turned a hobby into a business venture, created a unique product, or developed a new twist on an old theme. These all qualify as human-interest stories. Newspaper and magazine editors like them almost as much as their readers enjoy them.

Once you have your story angle, call the managing editor or the feature editor of your local newspaper. Give him or her a brief description of who you are and what business you are in. Say that you will be sending out a press release (see following sample) and would be happy to arrange an interview at a convenient time.

Sample Press Release

FOR IMMEDIATE RELEASE MORE INFORMATION
555-5555

NEW CATERING COMPANY

Katie Smith, owner of An Affair to Remember, is pleased to announce the opening of her new catering business, located on Union Street.

Smith worked for seven years as a head cook and pastry chef prior to starting An Affair to Remember.

"People today want to serve healthy, delicious food while entertaining, but don't have as much time as they once did to plan, shop, and cook," she says. "At some point, everyone entertains for friends, clients, or family. By bringing in a caterer for a birthday party, retirement dinner, or holiday luncheon, the host has an opportunity to *enjoy* the event and the company."

Smith wanted to share her expertise and love of cooking with a larger community, and give individual entertainers the opportunity to serve healthy, gourmet food to their guests.

If you would like to learn more about An Affair to Remember, contact Katie at 555-5555.

Invite journalists to visit your place of business to get a firsthand look at what you are doing and how you do it. Do the same with program directors or talk-show hosts at local and regional television and radio stations.

If, on the first attempt, your presentation fails to result in an article, follow up in three to six months, possibly with a new story angle. In the meantime, however, send out regular press releases announcing new developments with your business—the grand opening, special events, details on your business philosophy, extra services, and features.

Even if they don't run a full story on you, there is a good possibility you could be included in a feature story about local entrepreneurs or people in related businesses.

An Effective Ad Campaign

The advertisement is one of the most interesting and difficult of modern literary forms.

Aldous Huxley

All of the methods outlined earlier, along with any others you may develop, will keep your name in the consumer's mind. The effectiveness of an advertising and/or publicity campaign can be measured by conducting a simple marketing survey with new customers. Simply make it standard practice to ask each customer where he or she heard about you and your business.

Keep a tally of the responses in a notebook. A periodic review will give you hints of where to allocate future advertising funds. If, for example, the majority of your customers are being drawn from your display ad in the local newspaper, keep it going on a steady basis. The same principle applies to classified, direct-mail, or word-of-mouth advertising.

The justification for investing in advertising and promotion is time. If you attempted to contact all of the people who read ads and press-release material in newspapers, or those who listen to talk shows, you would never have time to conduct your business.

Time is money! As a small business owner, you will want to devote as much attention as possible to catering itself and let your advertising and promotion work bring in the customers.

In addition to the release about your catering business, you might offer two or three sample menus and possibly one or two popular recipes. Give *information* as often as possible. While there are no guarantees that your press release will get you any publicity, it's worth a try. Just make sure you target the release to an appropriate outlet.

Getting Started

At this point, you're ready to go out there and give the catering business a try. If you've done your homework, by now you should know

◆ What services you plan to provide

◆ What your prices will be for the services

◆ What your start-up costs and equipment needs are

◆ Several resources for recipes

◆ Some resources for equipment

◆ Where you will work—most likely home—and how to set up the space

◆ How to get started with advertising and promotion

It is absolutely crucial that you approach your start-up with good planning and organization. Take each step knowing what the previous step was and which step comes next. Likewise, know what you want to happen and what could happen; plan for problems, and have possible solutions ready.

This book just scratches the surface of the knowledge that you will want—and need—to acquire in the course of starting your business and making it grow. There are many resources to help you learn and stay abreast of the industry's latest news. Some of these resources follow in the Appendix.

Good luck to you in your new endeavor.

Notes

Personal Thoughts

Key Points

Additional Research

APPENDIX: RESOURCES

Associations and Agencies

Small Business Associations & Government Agencies

American Marketing Association
250 South Wacker Drive, Suite 200
Chicago, IL 60606-5819

Marketing publications available to nonmembers.

Bureau of the Census
Washington, DC 20233

Statistical data.

Chambers of Commerce
Consult Yellow Pages. Services vary among chambers but may include advice, support, workshops or seminars, local business news, and other services specifically for small businesses.

Council of Better Business Bureaus
4200 Wilson Boulevard, Suite 800
Arlington, VA 22203

Ask for a listing of their "Booklets on Wise Buying."

Dun & Bradstreet
299 Park Avenue
New York, NY 10171

Send for the booklet "This is Dun & Bradstreet," an overview
of publications and services.

Internal Revenue Service (IRS)
1-800-829-1040 General tax assistance
1-800-829-3676 Forms and publications

See the government section of your phone book for address
and phone of the local office. The IRS publishes a variety of
books and brochures that are useful to owners of small
businesses. Each year the IRS publishes "Tax Guide for Small
Business."

International Franchise Association
1350 New York Avenue NW
Washington, DC 20005

Regulation and information on franchises.

Local Planning Agencies
See the government section of your phone book for address
and phone of the local office. Source of information on zoning
and future development locations.

Minority Business Development Agency
Office of Public Affairs
Department of Commerce
Washington, DC 20230

National Association for the Self-Employed
P.O. Box 612067
DFW Airport, TX 75261-2067

National Association of Women Business Owners
600 South Federal Street
Chicago, IL 60605

National Federation of Independent Business
150 West 20th Avenue
San Mateo, CA 94403

National Insurance Consumer Organization
P.O. Box 3243
Merrifield, VA 22116-3243

Send $3 and self-addressed, stamped #10 envelope for booklet, "Buyer's Guide to Insurance."

National Minority Business Council
235 East 42nd Street
New York, NY 10017

Bimonthly newsletter for small and minority businesses.

National Small Business United
1155 15th Street NW, Suite 710
Washington, DC 20005

Send for information on federal legislation.

Occupational Safety & Health Administration (OSHA)
Department of Labor
200 Constitution Avenue
Washington, DC 20210

Employment regulations.

Office of Information and Public Affairs
U.S. Department of Labor
200 Constitution Avenue NW
Washington, DC 20210

Request publications list regarding employment.

Service Corps of Retired Executives (SCORE)
See Small Business Administration.

Small Buiness Administration
1441 L Street NW
Washington, DC 20416

The SBA is the primary source of federal governmental assistance for small businesses. In addition to providing financing for many small businesses, it provides a number of services for free or at a small cost. SBA regional offices routinely conduct free or low-cost small business workshops. The SBA also offers many helpful publications as well as the following hotlines:

SBA Answer Desk
Recorded information on a variety of topics

1-800-827-5722

SBA Online
A national electronic bulletin board service that provides an overview of SBA information.

1-800-859-INFO if you use a 2400 baud modem or 800-697-INFO if you use a 9600 baud modem

See also following entry.

Service Corps of Retired Executives (SCORE)
PO Box 15434
Fort Worth, TX 76119

Retired business executives offer their expertise and services to entrepreneurs through SBA's SCORE, which charges for out-of-pocket expenses but not for the consultant's time.

Telephone Company
Consult your local phone company. Most offer a variety of services and publications for small businesses.
AT&T 800-Number Information
Call 1-800-272-0400

Trade

Basic and Traditional Food Association
1707 "N" Street NW
Washington, DC 20036

Foodcrafters Guild
6003 North 51st Street
P.O. Box 2193
Boulder, CO 80306

Foodservice Consultants Society International
1800 Pickwick Avenue
Glenview, IL 60025

International Food Service Executives Association
111 E. Wacker Drive, Suite 600
Chicago, IL 60601
312-644-6610

National Association of Catering Executives
2500 Wilshire Blvd., Suite 603
Los Angeles, CA 90057
213-487-6223

National Institute of Off-Premise Catering
1341 N. Sedwick
Chicago, IL 60610
800-OFF-PREM

National Restaurant Association
311 1st Street NW
Washington, DC 20001
800-424-5156

Books

General Reference Books & Periodicals

Note: Many of the following resources are available through the Research Desk at your local library.

A Consumer's Guide to Telephone Service
Consumer Information Center, Pueblo, CO 81009

Bacon's Publicity Checker
A comprehensive listing of every major newspaper in the United States and Canada.

Directory of Publications and Broadcast Media
Published annually by Gale Research Company, Detroit, MI.

The Dun & Bradstreet Middle Market Directory
and *The Dun & Bradstreet Million Dollar Directory*
The Dun & Bradstreet Corporation, New York, NY

Encyclopedia of Associations
Published annually by Gale Research Company, Detroit, MI.

Encyclopedia of Business Information Sources
Published periodically by Gale Research Company, Detroit, MI.

Financial Studies of the Small Business
Financial Research Associates
PO Box 7708
Winter Haven, FL 33883

National Five-Digit ZIP Directory (2 volumes)
U.S. Postal Service
6060 Primacy Parkway, Suite 101
Memphis, TN 38188-0001

Also available by phone 1-800-238-3150 or through your local post office.

Poor's Register of Corporations, Directors, and Executives
New York, NY: Standard & Poor's Corporation

Roget's Thesaurus in Dictionary Form
New York: HarperCollins, 1992

Synonyms and antonyms.

Tax Guide for Small Businesses
Internal Revenue Service publication. Published annually.
Available from local IRS office.

Thomas Register of American Manufacturers
Thomas Publishing Company, New York, NY

Ulrich's International Periodicals Directory
Comprehensive listing of major magazines and newspapers.

Webster's New Collegiate Dictionary
Springfield, MA: G & C Merriam Company, 1989

Where to Find Business Information
by David Brownstone and Gorton Carruth
New York: John Wiley & Sons, 1982

Magazines

General Business

Business Marketing
Crain Communications, Inc.
740 N. Rush Street
Chicago, IL 60611

Published monthly.

Entrepreneur Magazine
2392 Morse Avenue
Irvine, CA 92714

Published monthly.

Sales & Marketing Management
Bill Communications, Inc.
355 Park Avenue South
New York, NY 10010

Published monthly except in June, August, and October, when
it is published twice a month.

Success, The Magazine for Today's Entrepreneurial Mind
Lang Communications
230 Park Avenue
New York, NY 10169

Published monthly with the exception of bimonthly issues for January/February and July/August.

Trade

Bon Appétit
360 Madison Avenue
New York, NY 10017

Cooking Light
P.O. Box 830656
Birmingham, AL 35282-9056
800-336-0125

Food & Wine
New York, NY
800-333-6569

Gourmet Magazine
560 Lexington Avenue
New York, NY 10022

Saveur
800-234-5118

Taunton's Fine Cooking
The Taunton Press, Inc.
Newton, CT 06470-5506
203-426-8171

Vegetarian Times
800-435-9610

INDEX

A

Accounting services, 103, 129
Ad response, tracking and
 predicting, 213-216
Adult education, 13, 26, 190
Advertising, 205-217. *See also*
 Promotion
 effective, 115, 224-225
 publications for, 74
 results of, 217
 types of, 206-213
Advertising Research
 Foundation, 217
American Free Enterprise
 System, 4
Appearance advertising, 206-207
Assets, analyzing, 128
Association of Business
 Publishers, 217
Attitude, importance of, 192
Attorney, lease review by, 57, 97

Auctions, buying equipment at,
 53, 54
Audience, identifying, 73. *See
 also* Clients; Customers

B

Balance sheet, 128, 147, 153, 154
 personal, 136
Bank loans, 133-134, 135-136
Bankruptcy, 4
Bank statement, reconciling,
 147, 154-155
Banquet manager, 196
Better Business Bureau, 53
Bidding, 170
Bookkeeping, 103, 147-148,
 149-150. *See also* Record
 keeping
Bookkeeping systems,
 standardized, 148
Brainstorming, 116, 222
Break-even analysis, 159-160
Brochures, 70, 220

U

Undercapitalization, 131. *See also* Financing
Unit price, calculating, 163
Used equipment, 51, 52-53
Utilities, 91

V

Vehicles, delivery, 57-58
Vendors, information from, 76
Venture capitalists, 137-138
Visitors, limiting, 185
Voice mail, 92-93

W

Wages, personal, 161
Warranties, equipment, 53
WATS line, 93
Weight Watchers, 86
Wholesale businesses, 96
Wholesale prices, 163-164
Windows, 40
Word-of-mouth advertising, 207
Work orders, 155
Work schedule, establishing, 89
Work space, layout of, 85
Writing, of display ads, 209-210

Y

Yellow Pages advertising, 212-213

Z

Zoning ordinances, 85, 90, 91